Pro-Life

Pro-Life
Defending the Culture of Life against the Culture of Death

iUniverse, Inc.

For information address:
iUniverse, Inc.
2021 Pine Lake Road, Suite 100
Lincoln, NE 68512
www.iuniverse.com

ISBN: 0-595-29779-X

Printed in the United States of America

Dedicated to Christianity's greatest disciples, Pro-lifers

The Kingdom of God is yours.
Well done my good and faithful servants.

Contents

Preface

Father Frank Pavone, the founder of Priests for Life, was praying outside an abortion clinic with a picture of Our Lady of Guadalupe present in his midst. Suddenly, a woman left the clinic and came to the sidewalk counselors and sought information. She cancelled her abortion and received help from the pro-life community. She gave birth to a beautiful baby girl whom Fr. Pavone baptized with the name Guadalupe.

It is entirely appropriate that the cover of this book depicts the traditional pro-life image of Our Lady of Guadalupe, for to truly understand life in all its fullness we must explore the mystery of Mary, the mother of Jesus, the source of all authentic and full life.

It was the sixteenth century and the situation in what is now known as Mexico was reaching the boiling point. The Spaniards and the Aztecs had a profound hate for each other, so much so, that the Aztecs were preparing to mount a revolt against them. Many of the Spanish viewed the Aztecs as less than human and despised their very presence. The Aztecs felt they were being enslaved and being culturally destroyed. They hated everything Spanish, their culture, their religion, and their very being. In preparation for this military assault the Aztecs increased their religious practice of human sacrifices.

On December 12, 1531 the Blessed Mother appeared to an Aztec named Juan Diego. In order to convince the bishop of the truth of the apparition, the Blessed Mother, Our Lady of Guadalupe, asked Juan to go to the top of a hill which was covered with frost and had never grown anything but cacti. To his surprise he found perfectly formed Castillian roses. Placing them in his tilma (a form of poncho) he brought the roses to the bishop. When he opened his tilma, the roses fell to the ground and the image of Our Lady of Guadalupe miraculously appeared on the tilma.

From this moment onward the conversion of the Spanish and Aztecs began. Human sacrifices ended, the Catholic faith was accepted, and the Spanish and Aztecs would come together and become the Mexican race, the Mexican people.

Our Lady of Guadalupe saves lives and gives dignity to all, through her son Jesus Christ.

Holy Mary, Mother of God, pray for us sinners now and at the hour of our death! Our Lady of Victory, pray for us! Patroness of the Unborn, pray for us!

Let us respond to God as Mary responded to God's messenger: "Let it be done according to your will" (Luke 1:38).

Foreword

As the Spiritual Moderator for the Diocese of Palm Beach's Respect Life Office, I experienced what I had never experienced in all my life, absolute evil.

I found it in police officers who spent their off-time as paid employees for abortion mills, arresting people, including handicapped people, for simply and accidentally crossing unto abortion mill property. I have seen whole parking lots closed to parking because of the intimidation tactics of abortion facilities. I have seen jumping and dancing abortion escorts as young teenagers came into their parking lots to seek out an abortion. I have seen sidewalk counselors arrested for simply trying to give women information, which is denied to them in abortion mills. I have been threatened, yelled at, mocked, and spate upon, for simply praying the Rosary on a sidewalk. I have seen the rejection of pro-life bulletin boards for simply displaying an accurate depiction of an unborn child's ear; only unrealistic, earless children were acceptable. I have experienced the hostility of local newspapers to the culture of life and even the rejection of *paid* pro-life ads in their so-called objective newspapers: You can place an ad promoting all kinds of decadence, but don't you dare try to place a pro-life or a pro culture of life ad. I read letters of abortion clinic managers that unhesitatingly admitted that human beings were being aborted in their clinics, but since it was legal it was okay. I have been demeaned and publicly humiliated by so-called objective television interviewers and reporters for defending the dignity of the person from conception to natural death.

If one does not believe in the devil and the power of evil, I simply ask you to take up the cause of defending the culture of life and you will experience pure evil. The fires of hell will awaken! Beware! Be prepared!

Introduction:
A Loving, Forgiving People

There is no love or compassion without truth.

We as people of truth must seek to embrace and nourish the "culture of life" amidst a "culture of death." We as people are called to promote and defend the sanctity of life from conception to natural death through a life of prayer, service, and education.

The "culture of death," under the guise of good, assaults the dignity of the person through abortion, embryonic stem-cell research, cloning, and other forms of destructive biological engineering. The dignity of the person is battered by poverty, crime, and disenfranchisement, and it is shattered through the death penalty and euthanasia. When the dignity of the person is compromised at any stage, and in any manner, a society is bound to disintegrate.

There is no love or compassion without truth.

1

Margaret Sanger, Founder, Mother, and Prophet of the Culture of Death

Margaret Sanger, the darling and heroine of Planned Parenthood, could never have dreamed that her deepest desires would be fulfilled in our time. And because of this reality, Sanger can rightly be acknowledged as the "Founder, Mother, and Prophet of the Culture of Death."

Margaret Sanger was born in Corning, New York, on September 14, 1879. She began her career as a nurse in White Plains, New York. While working as a nurse and among the poor some force changed the course of her life. She would abandon nursing and devote herself to the promotion of contraception and ultimately abortion.

In 1916 she established the first American birth-control clinic in Brooklyn, New York. She began publishing her gospel through her magazine *Birth Control Review* and founded in 1921 the American Birth Control League. In 1927 she organized the World Population Conference and in 1942 she became the chairperson of the Planned Parenthood Federation of America, which was formed from the American Birth Control League.

Margaret Sanger sought to convert the United States to the religion of eugenics under the guise of social progress and the betterment of humanity. She felt that eugenics was the "most adequate avenue to the solution of racial, political, and social problems." And how was this to be done? And what were her goals? **Let her own words speak for her and her disciples:**

- *"We should hire three or four colored ministers, preferably with social-service backgrounds, and with engaging personalities. The most successful educational approach to the Negro is through a religious appeal. We don't want the word*

1

to get out that we want to exterminate the Negro population, and the minister is the man who can straighten out that idea if it ever occurs to any of their more rebellious members" (Letter to Dr. Clarence Gamble, Sophia Smith Collection, Smith College).

- "Our failure to segregate morons who are increasing and multiplying...demonstrates our foolhardy and extravagant sentimentalism...[Philanthropists] encourage the healthier and more normal sections of the world to shoulder the burden of the unthinking and indiscriminate fecundity of others; which brings with it, as I think the reader must agree, a dead weight of human waste. Instead of decreasing and aiming to eliminate the stocks that are most detrimental to the future of the race and the world, it tends to render them to a menacing degree dominant...We are paying for, and even submitting to, the dictates of an ever-increasing, unceasingly spawning class of human beings who never should have been born at all" (The Pivot of Civilization, "The Cruelty of Charity," Swarthmore College Library Edition, 116, 122, 189).

- "I think you must agree...that the campaign for birth control is not merely of eugenic value, but is practically identical with the final aims of eugenics...Birth control propaganda is thus the entering wedge for the eugenic educator...As an advocate of birth control I wish...to point out that the unbalance between the birth rate of the 'unfit' and the 'fit,' admittedly the greatest present menace to civilization, can never be rectified by the inauguration of a cradle competition between these two classes. In this matter, the example of the inferior classes, the fertility of the feeble-minded, the mentally defective, the poverty-stricken classes, should not be held up for emulation...On the contrary, the most urgent problem today is how to limit and discourage the over-fertility of the mentally and physically defective" (Birth Control Review, "The Eugenic Value of Birth Control Propaganda," October 1921, 5).

- "Give dysgenic groups [people with 'bad genes'] in our population their choice of segregation or [compulsory] sterilization" (Birth Control Review, April 1932).

- "The third group [of society] are those irresponsible and reckless ones having little regard for the consequences of their acts, or whose religious scruples prevent their exercising control over their numbers. Many of this group are diseased, feeble-minded, and are of the pauper element dependent upon the normal and fit members of society for their support. There is no doubt in the minds of all thinking people that the procreation of this group should be stopped" (Birth Control Review, "What It Is, How It Works, What It Will Do," Gothic Press, 172).

- *"In passing, we should here recognize the difficulties presented by the idea of 'fit' and 'unfit.' Who is to decide this question? The grosser, the more obvious, the undeniably feeble-minded should, indeed, not only be discouraged but prevented from propagating their kind. But among the writings of the representative eugenists, one cannot ignore the distinct middle-class bias that prevails"* (Family Planning Perspectives, January-February, 1985, 44).

- *"[There should be] more children from the fit, less from the unfit"* (Birth Control Review, vol. 3, no. 5, May 1919, 2).

- *"There is only one reply to a request for a higher birthrate among the intelligent, and that is to ask the government to first take the burden of the insane and feeble-minded from your back. [Mandatory] sterilization for these is the answer"* (Birth Control Review, October 1926).

- *"Birth control must lead ultimately to a cleaner race"* (Women, Morality, and Birth Control, New York Publishing Co., 1922, 12).

- *"[Slavs, Latin, and Hebrew immigrants are] human weeds...a deadweight of human waste...[Black, soldiers, and Jews are a] menace to the race" "Eugenic sterilization is an urgent need...We must prevent multiplication of this bad stock"* (Birth Control Review, April 1933).

- *"[Our objective is] unlimited sexual gratification without the burden of unwanted children...[Women must have the right] to live...to love...to be lazy...to be an unmarried mother...to create...to destroy...The marriage bed is the most degenerate influence in the social order...The most merciful thing that a family does to one of its infant members is to kill it"* (The Woman Rebel, Volume 1, Number 1, reprinted in Woman in the New Race New York, Brentanos Publishers, 1922).

And what was Sanger's "Plan for Peace," (*Birth Control Review*, vol. 16, no. 4, April 1932).

1. *"To keep the doors of immigration closed to the entrance of certain aliens whose condition is known to be detrimental to the stamina of the race, such as the feebleminded as determined by Stanford Binet I.Q. tests."*

2. *"To apply a stern and rigid policy of sterilization and segregation to that grade of population whose progeny is already tainted, or whose inheritance is such that objectionable traits may be transmitted to offspring."*

3. *"To insure the country against future burdens of maintenance for numerous offspring as may be born of feeble-minded parents by pensioning all persons with transmissible diseases who voluntarily consent to sterilization."*

4.   *"To give dysgenic groups in our population their choice of segregation or ster-ilization."*

5.   *"To apportion farm lands and homesteads for these segregated persons where they would be taught to work under competent instructors for a period of their entire lives."*

6.   *"Take an inventory of the secondary group such as illiterates, paupers, unemployables, criminals, prostitutes, dope fiends; classify them in special departments under government medical protection, and segregate them on farms and open spaces as long as necessary for the strengthening and develop-ment of moral conduct."*

As you read the essays in this book you will be shockingly surprised at how evilly prophetic her words were and continue to be!

Margaret Sanger died in 1966 having given birth to the legacy of the "culture of death." One can reasonably argue that she became the founder, mother, and prophet of the culture of death.

2

Personhood

If you were to ask any embryologist when life begins, you would hear without hesitation: "Life begins when a human ovum is fertilized by a human spermatozoa. That is, life begins at syngamy when a one-celled zygote is produced. At syngamy a human organism, a member of the human species, comes into existence." In other words, in terms we can understand, human life begins at conception (syngamy).

At conception we have a human organism, a human being. We do not have a baboon organism or a chimpanzee organism or an elephant organism. With few exceptions, there is a general consensus on this point.

Having said this, however, one may ask: "If this is so, why is it that abortion, stem-cell research on embryos, and all kinds of experimentations on embryos is permitted to take place?"

The answer to this is based upon an ancient pagan theory that is often today referred to as the theory of "delayed hominization." This theory essentially maintains that one can be a human organism without being a human person. And so, for some scientists, ethicists, and moralists if one is not a human person then one does not have the rights of a human person.

The great dilemma that arises from such a view is: When does one become a person? For some individuals, one becomes a person at approximately two weeks after conception when the embryo is implanted in the uterus; for others it is at three weeks when the heart is beating, or at six weeks when brain waves are measurable and the child moves and responds to touch, or at eight weeks when the body is completely formed, or at twelve weeks when all organ systems are functioning, or at twenty weeks at viability (when the child can live outside the womb), or at birth, or at infancy, or at four to six years of age. That's right. At birth, infancy, and four to six years of age.

The Nobel Prize winning co-discoverer of the DNA double helix, Francis Crick, believes that if a child is born with a defect, then a mother should have the right to euthanize (kill) the child within the first two to three days of birth (NCCB, *Life-Insights*, March-April, 2001). The so-called scholar Tristram Engelhardt Jr. maintains that one is not a human person until one is able to experience abstract thought and reflective self-consciousness (*Foundations of Bioethics*, 1986).

Does this remind you of anything? This hideous and false vision of life has tragic consequences, for if one can assign personhood by an arbitrary standard, then one can take away personhood accordingly by an arbitrary standard.

In the early years of this country, slavery was justified on the grounds that slaves were considered property and not persons. In Nazi Germany the handicapped, the seriously ill, the gypsies, and finally the Jews and all who opposed Nazism were exterminated for failing to be authentic Aryan persons. As the Nazis would say of the handicapped War World I veterans before they were exterminated: "These are useless eaters."

If you take a person's personhood away, you can do almost anything to a person. When one plays with a person's personhood all kinds of egregious acts are in the shadows waiting to come out.

Since many Alzheimer's patients and many mentally handicapped individuals are incapable of abstract thought and self-reflection, are they to be put to death for not being persons? Sadly to say this is occurring in many western countries! How many persons can we think of who are not worthy of being assigned personhood? How many persons can we think of who should have had their personhood taken away from them? This is the slippery slope to hell!

For the Catholic, one is a human being and a human person from the moment of conception. There is no separating of the two! As Pope John Paul II clarifies in the Gospel of Life: "How can one be a human being without being a human person?" Or as the ecclesiastical writer of the third century, Tertullian, wrote: "one becomes a human person only because one already is a human person."

At the moment of conception a person's sex, facial features, body type, hair, eye, and skin color are determined. Even a person's future intelligence and personality are influenced by the genetic code present at conception. Every aspect of who and what a person is is present from the beginning of human life with the exception of the exercise of free will, time to grow and mature, and the influences of the environment. What I am at 40 is what I was at conception with the exception of the exercise of my will, time to grow and mature, and environmental influences. Everything I will be at 67 is what I am now at 40, with the same exceptions.

From the moment of conception, we are simultaneously human beings and human persons.

Let no one take your personhood away from you or anyone else. Be vigilant, for one day they might come after you and take away your personhood.

3

Just the Facts

A woman seeking an abortion before the fourteenth week of pregnancy will likely undergo one of the following procedures:

Suction Curettage

1. The cervix is dilated.

2. A suction curette (a hollow tube with a knife-like edged tip) is inserted into the womb.

3. Suction tears apart the fetus (the human person) and sucks the body parts into a container.

4. The container is checked to assure that all the body parts have been removed in order to prevent any infections—infections which can at times lead to the death of the mother.

Dilation and Curettage (D&C)

1. The cervix is dilated.

2. The insertion of a loop-shaped knife (curette) is inserted.

3. The curette scrapes the wall of the uterus and cuts the placenta and fetus into smaller parts.

4. The parts are pulled out of the uterus through the cervix.

5. Body parts must be counted so as to prevent infection.

RU 486 (taken before the ninth week)

1. A steroid drug (taken in the form of a pill or injection) is given to the woman to destroy the placenta or prevent it from being formed.

2. Prostaglandin is injected or orally given to induce the uterus to contract and push the fetus out of the body.

During the first fourteen weeks brain waves (week six) are recorded and the heart is beating (week three). The child can hear, can hiccup, can close and open his eyelids and can respond to touch or pain. The child has permanent fingerprints and an identifiable sex. By week eight the skeletal, nervous, digestive, circulatory, and respiratory system are functioning. By week twelve the child looks like a tiny doll sucking its thumb. The following weeks entail simple refinements of what has already begun.

Pagans routinely aborted their children and abandoned them to die outside city walls. We have outdone the pagans in our cruelty. The revival of paganism is more vicious than its original incarnation.

A woman seeking an abortion after fourteen weeks but before sixteen weeks of pregnancy will likely undergo the following procedure:

Dilation and Evacuation (D&E)

1. The cervix is dilated.

2. A curette (resembling pliers) is used to dismember and crush the large and strong bones of the fetus (such as the skull or head).

3. The dismembered and crushed parts are now small enough for removal through the cervix.

4. Body parts are counted.

A woman seeking an abortion after sixteen weeks of pregnancy will likely undergo one of the following procedures:

Saline Solution Evacuation

1. A concentrated salt solution is injected through the abdomen and into the amniotic fluid, which surrounds the fetus (the child) in the uterus.

2. The child inhales and swallows the solution and dies within two hours either by salt poisoning, dehydration, hemorrhaging, or convulsions.

3. The mother goes into labor twenty-four to forty-eight hours later and gives birth to a dead child.

Prostaglandin Abortion

1. Prostaglandin is injected through the abdomen into the amniotic fluid, which surrounds the child in the uterus.

2. Prostaglandin causes the muscle tissue of the mother to push the fetus, the child, out of the uterus.

3. The child is born dead or alive (when born alive it is left to die).

A woman seeking an abortion during the latter periods of her pregnancy will likely undergo the following procedure:

Partial-Birth Abortion or Dilation and Extraction

1. Laminara is used to dilate the cervix over a two-day period.

2. The abortionist uses large forceps to grasp the leg of the child (the fetus) and pulls it down into the vagina and out of the body. The head, being too big, remains lodged in the cervical opening.

3. An incision is made at the base of the fetal skull to spread open the skull in order to insert a suction catheter.

4. The skull contents are evacuated through the suction catheter and the entire body is now capable of being removed.

These atrocious acts take place everyday in the United States.

At approximately seven weeks of pregnancy, when the heart, brain, stomach, liver, and kidney are functioning, 800,000 infants are aborted each year. At sixteen weeks when the child's organs are complete and functioning and the child is breathing (fluid), swallowing, digesting, sleeping, dreaming, and experiencing pleasure and pain, 71,000 American babies are aborted each year.

First-trimester aborted babies are disposed of by flushing them down a garbage disposal or "Insinkerator," or disposed of in biological waste bags. Larger bodies are often sold for research purposes. Third-trimester babies are often disposed of in on-site crematoria. In the most egregious cases, full-term babies have been burned alongside of dogs, cats, and birds and thrown out by local Humane society offices (Clowes, *Facts of Life*, 15). Some have even gone so far as to use meat grinders and garbage disposals (Ibid., 15).

Abortion is the number one killer of Americans. In 1997's CDC report, heart disease claimed approximately 725,000 lives, cancer 530,000, stroke 150,000, pulmonary disease 110,000, diabetes 62,000, suicide 30,000, nephritic syndrome

25,000, kidney disease 25,000, AIDS 22,000, and accidents 92,000. On the other hand, in terms of abortion, anywhere from 1.3 to 1.4 million babies are aborted each year. Some 4,000 infants are aborted each day, one every twenty-two seconds.

Forty-five abortions a day are performed on women in America who are five month or more into their pregnancy. Forty-three percent of women who have abortions will have two or more. While the average abortion takes five to ten minutes, the average wait to adopt a child is two to ten years.

In the World Trade Center terrorist attack, over 3,000 individuals died. This led to a war against terrorism and a war in Iraq. Some 3,800 to 4,500 abortions take place every day in this country. Why are we not as outraged at these abortions as we were at the World Trade Center catastrophe? Why are we not as determined to put an end to abortion as we are to terrorism?

The total number of Americans who have been killed in American wars in the name of freedom and dignity is 1,178,863 (Revolutionary War, 25,324; War of 1812, 2,260; Mexican War, 13,283; Civil War, 498,332; Spanish-American War, 2,446; WWI, 116,708; WWII, 407,316; Korean War, 54,246; Vietnam War, 58,655; Persian Gulf War I, 293; Persian Gulf War II, undetermined).

Why have we failed to give the same dignity and freedom to forty million aborted children that we have sought, sacrificed, and fought to give to others?

"Woe to you, Chorazin. Woe to you, Bethsaida" (Luke 10:13).

Awaken us, O Lord. May we see as you see and hear as you hear. May we bring your love to the world and create it anew.

4

The Pill, the Silent Abortion

If we were to ask most couples about the negative side effects associated with the use of the pill, most couples would have a general idea regarding these effects, either through information obtained from their doctors or from pharmacists. They may not be aware of the fifty-two side effects associated with the use of the pill, but they more than likely would be aware of the most talked about side effects such as strokes, heart attacks, and blood clots.

If, however, we were to ask most couples about the method in which the pill works in preventing the birth of children, there would be a tremendous amount of ignorance.

There are two major types of pills that are being used in preventing the birth of children: those that contain a combination of estrogen and progestogen and those that contain only progestogen. Both of these types of pills prevent the birth of children either through preventing ovulation or preventing the effective migration of sperm in the uterus, or by preventing implantation. In the Physicians' Desk Reference the combination pills are described as operating in the following manner: "Combination oral contraceptives act by suppression of gonadotropins. Although the primary mechanism of this action is the inhibition of ovulation, other alterations include changes in the cervical mucus (which increase the difficulty of sperm entry into the uterus) and the endometrium (which reduce the likelihood of implantation)."

In terms of the progestogen-only pill, the Physicians' Desk Reference states: "[Progestogen-only pills] alter cervical mucus, exert a progestational effect on the endometrium, interfering with implantation, and in some patients, suppress ovulation."

Therefore, the pill (whether the combination pill or the progestogen-only pill) has the potential for being an abortifacient—an abortion-causing agent. When conception takes place, a human being is present. The pill at this point, because it weakens the lining of the uterus, prevents this human being from being implanted in the womb of the mother.

This is a silent abortion. As the Church teaches in its documents, and in particular in the 1994 American document *Ethical and Religious Directives for Catholic Health Care Services* (n. 45): "Every procedure whose sole immediate effect is the termination of pregnancy before viability is an abortion, which, in its moral context, includes the interval between conception and implantation of the embryo."

What is said of the "pill" can be said, with slight variations, on all the other hormonal methods of contraception including Norplant, Depo-Provera, RU-486 and Ovral.

Similar abortifacient effects are also apparent in the use of intrauterine devices such as Lippes Loop and the Copper-T 380A.

How many silent victims are being lost because of the unknowing actions of couples? Who is at fault for their ignorance?

5

Natural Family Planning

The use of contraceptives is intrinsically evil. As *Familiaris Consortio*, 32, explains regarding the evil of contraceptives and the contraceptive attitude:

"The innate language that expresses the total reciprocal self-giving of husband and wife is overlaid, through contraception, by an objectively contradictory language, namely, that of not giving oneself totally to the other. This leads not only to a positive refusal to be open to life but also to a falsification of the inner truth of conjugal love, which is called upon to give itself in personal totality... The difference, both anthropological and moral, between contraception and recourse to the rhythm of the cycle...involves in the final analysis two irreconcilable concepts of the human person and of human sexuality."

The old fashion "calendar-rhythm" method, which was highly inaccurate and inadequate, is no longer the means used for natural family planning. Today the methods of determining a woman's fertile period has become more sophisticated and accurate. Some prefer the use of the Ovulation-Billings method, others prefer the Symtpo-Thermal method.

The following is a description of the Billings method for discovering the time of ovulation:

1. *"The menstrual period at the start of each cycle is considered to be fertile. The reason for viewing the time of menstruation as fertile is that if a woman should have an unusually or unexpectedly short cycle such that the ovulation process were to begin toward the end of menstruation, she would have no warning of this fact, since the presence of the menstrual flow would make it difficult for her to examine her vaginal mucus. Thus, as a precaution, women are advised to regard the menstrual period as fertile.*

2. *After menstruation there is a noticeable absence of any vaginal discharge or mucus, and a woman experiences a definite sensation of dryness. During these days of dryness, the woman is infertile.*

3. *At the conclusion of this period of dryness, cervical mucus begins to be discharged from the vagina. At first, this mucus is a kind of cloudy, sticky discharge, but it gradually becomes a clear, egg-white, stretchy, and lubricative substance. The "peak" or main sign of ovulation is the last day on which this clear and stretchy mucus is present. The woman's period of fertility, however, is defined as starting with the first day on which the cloudy mucus appears and it continues until three days past the peak symptom of ovulation.*

4. *Finally, from the fourth day after the peak symptom until the start of the next menstrual cycle, a period of infertility occurs" (Genovesi, Catholic Morality and Human Sexuality, 229)."*

The Sympto-Thermal method combines, in the words of Dr. Brian Clowes, *"observations of basal body temperature and cervical mucus, and, as an optional cross-check, adds an examination of the cervical os (mouth of the cervix) as well. During fertile periods, the os opens, the cervix rises, and its tip becomes softer…During infertile times, the os closes, the cervix descends, and the tip becomes firmer…The end of pre-ovulation infertility is determined in several different ways. As a general rule, couples may resume intercourse on the fourth day following the peak day of mucus and the third day of upward thermal shift…Every time that a fertile type of mucus appears before ovulation, they must abstain for three days. Once ovulation occurs, the couple is sterile until menstruation and usually sterile during the fist two days of menstruation"* (Facts of Life, 95).

Obviously the above are fragmentary summaries of the methods used for natural family planning. But the hope is that the above descriptions give couples an idea of the methods for natural family planning, and that they may seek their local parish ministry office and sign up for a course on natural family planning.

Those who practice one of these methods of natural family planning have a less than one in eight chance of divorcing as opposed to those who use contraceptives. Contraceptive users have over a fifty percent divorce rate. The reasons are simple.

1. NFP methods are natural. That is, they do not hinder the natural functioning of the body but observes and respects the natural cycle of fertility and infertility.

2. These methods respect the bodies of the spouses, encourage tenderness, and foster the necessary freedom that is at the base of authentic self-giving love.

3. In the practice of living out the natural methods one is engaging in a love which is expressed by the husband in saying, "I give you everything I am without doubt, without reservation, fully and completely," and the wife in turn says to her husband, "I give you my very self, completely, fully, without doubt, and without reservation." It is only in this grace-filled experience that the Gospel call of two becoming one can be fulfilled (cf. Mark 10:6-9).

4. Human life and the duty of transmitting it in cooperation with God is a spiritual gift that is not limited to this life's horizons, but has its true evaluation and full significance in reference to one's eternal destiny.

Those who practice natural family planning, as opposed to artificial contraception, make the sex act a spiritual act, a unitive, bonding, and creative act.

6

Post-Abortion Trauma

Trauma, if not dealt with, will manifest itself in the most negative of ways. Hence, the trauma of abortion, if not dealt with, will wreak havoc on a woman and consequently on much of society.

Women who have had abortions often seek to deal with the pain in essentially four manners: through suppression, repression, rationalization, and/or compensation (cf. Theresa Burke, Ph.D., *Forbidden Grief*, 2002).

Suppression

Women who seek to suppress the trauma of abortion consciously push away or push down any negative feelings. They do everything possible not to think about the abortion or its trauma. These are women who often turn to alcohol or drugs to numb their pain, or become workaholics to keep busy and distracted, or avoid prayer, church, and God. It is not unusual to notice a person get up and walk out of church when the very word abortion is mentioned. They are not being disrespectful. They are simply avoiding a reminder of their trauma.

In the most extreme cases, women who suppress their pain will often have more than one abortion (three to ten is not unusual) with the hope that each abortion will lessen the trauma (forty-five percent of women who have had an abortion, will have more than one). The mentality is: "The more I have, the less it will hurt."

Repression

Women who repress the trauma of abortion do so without any conscious awareness. Repression is a subconscious defense mechanism where the mind blocks out any negativity. These repressed feelings manifest themselves through an inability to bond with their husbands or children and an inability to form deep relationships.

Repression also manifests itself in certain disorders and unexplained actions. A woman went in for counseling because of lingering depression. The woman was astonishingly beautiful with the exception of her hair. It was so short that a comb could not pass through it. After months of therapy, the mystery was uncovered. The woman's hair was so short because she could not bear to hear the sound of a hair dryer. It reminded her of the suction catheter used during her abortion. Likewise, through therapy, another woman was able to recognize that the only reason she had replaced all her carpets in her home with wood flooring, was that the sound of the vacuum cleaner reminded her of the suction catheter used in her abortion. These women were doing things they could not explain because they were subconsciously trying to deal with the trauma of abortion. It was through therapy that what was being repressed came to light.

Rationalization

At a local abortion facility, while a group of pro-life individuals were gently and lovingly praying the Rosary, a woman volunteer from the clinic drove into the parking lot, jumped out of her car, and ran over to confront a woman praying. She was so filled with anger and malice that her body shook as she screamed.

This is a classic example of the coping mechanism of rationalization at work. Rationalization is an argument that one makes to justify one's action as acceptable. It is marked with intolerance, anger, and hatred. If I were a betting man, I would bet that this volunteer had had an abortion at some time in her life.

The rationalization of many women who have had an abortion is that "if it is legal, it must be OK." Therefore, any threat to the legal status of abortion is a threat to their coping with the trauma.

This is the same rationalization that is behind the efforts to eliminate the "Choose Life" plates in Florida. These plates are a threat to the legal status of abortion.

Compensation

Compensation is a coping mechanism that seeks to "make up" for past mistakes. Often women feel they must be punished in order to compensate for the evil of their abortion. This manifests itself in self-mutilation, suicide, anorexia, bulimia, and a wide range of self-punishing behaviors.

This compensation mechanism is often seen in what is known as the "perfect mother syndrome." Mothers often try to make up for what they did to their first child by trying to be the perfect mother for their subsequent children.

They can often become doting and controlling parents in their efforts to make everything perfect.

The reality of post-abortion trauma and its manifestation can in no way be completely described in such a short essay. Book after book has been written about this subject. But my hope is simply to illustrate one small portion of the damage that is done to women in the name of abortion and so-called women's rights.

Let us make no mistake about it. Those who support abortion have no love for women.

7

Post-Abortion Trauma, A Family Affair

Women, Mothers

The trauma that women experience after having had an abortion will take many forms and may appear immediately after the abortion or some forty years afterwards. One way or another, a woman's life will never be the same, either at a very conscious level or a subconscious level.

Women experience overwhelming feelings of guilt, isolation, grief, anger, depression, and shame. They often develop obsessive compulsive disorders and various forms of addictive behaviors such as eating disorders, and alcohol and drug abuse. Women often feel alienated from God and from the Church. At times they feel anger at God and the sense that they can never be forgiven.

Men, Fathers

Men are often haunted by nightmares about their unborn children. They often develop feelings of great guilt, remorse, sadness, and powerlessness. They often punish themselves by forms of self abuse such as alcoholism, drug use, or bodily mutilations (i.e., extensive piercings and tattoos). At times men can turn feelings of betrayal, powerlessness, and loss of trust into acts of aggression and abuse toward women. Men often seek to run away from these feelings by leaving their partners. It is not unusual that an abortion marks the end of a relationship.

Siblings

Siblings are often afflicted by despair, confusion, and a general fear of the world. Because of repressed or subconscious anger, children of mothers who have had abortions have a higher rate of being physically abused. Siblings often suffer what is known as "Survivor Syndrome," which is a mixture of anger and guilt associated with the overwhelming feeling of "why did I survive and my brother or sister didn't?" At times siblings feel that somehow their existence has caused the death of their sibling: "Mom and Dad could only handle one of us!" And in some cases children develop a paralyzing fear of their mothers, for they feel that "I might be next to get rid of."

Grandparents

Grandparents often experience many of the above symptoms of post-abortion trauma, but most feel a sense of anger, bitterness, resentment, depression and despair over the abortion. Often they feel unable to forgive their daughter or step-daughter. Most often, whether at a conscious or subconscious level, grandparents experience an un-repairable strain on their relationship with their daughter or step-daughter.

Abortion is a family tragedy and a societal tragedy. The more we permit the continuance of abortion, the more the family will die out. When the family structure dies, the culture will die, society will die, and eventually the world will enter into an age of anarchy. Are we now witnessing the death of Western civilization? Are we at the dawn of a new age of heathenism?

Those who suffer from the trauma of abortion can seek help through several healing programs provided by churches and certain psychologists and psychiatrists. Two of the most famous Catholic Post-Abortion healing ministries are Rachel's Vineyard and Project Rachel—PACE is the Protestant counterpart. In God all can be healed.

8

Abortion and the African-American Community

Abortion is the leading cause of death in the African-American community. Since 1973 to the present 695,000 African-Americans have died from AIDS, 206,313 from violent crimes, 370,723 from accidents, 1,638,350 from cancer, 2,266,789 from heart disease and 13 million from abortion. Abortion dwarfs all the major causes of death in the African-American community (US Center for Disease Control). Is this a coincidence?

Margaret Sanger, the founder of Planned Parenthood, the leading provider of abortion services, wrote to a colleague, Clarence Gamble in 1939: *"The "poorer areas, particularly in the South…are producing alarmingly more than their share of future generations. We do not want the word to get out that we want to exterminate the Negro population"* (*Smith Collection*, Smith College).

Is it a coincidence that a disproportionate number of abortion clinics in the United States are located in minority neighborhoods? Is it a coincidence that thirty-five percent of abortions are performed on African-American women, while they only represent twelve percent of the female population (US CDC/US Census Bureau). Is it a coincidence that more African-Americans have died from abortion than any other cause?

Planned Parenthood was founded with evil intentions, and what is founded on evil most often continues to foster evil. While many current members of Planned Parenthood may not be racists per se, they do, however, work with an organization that in its inception systematically and deliberately sought to hinder the growth and success of any non-Caucasian race.

Human life is sacred for it "involves the creative action of God and it remains for ever in a special relationship with the Creator (CCC 2258). Every human being bears the handprint of God, the image and likeness of his or her Creator.

God sees and loves in us what he sees and loves in his Son, Jesus Christ. Any act that diminishes the dignity of any human person is a direct assault on God, a direct assault on his image and likeness, his very presence in the core of every human being. An act of racism is an act of hatred toward God.

Racism is a cancer that destroys the fabric of society, and abortion providers are among the leading proponents of this type of racism in the African-American community, whether they are aware of it or not.

9

Breast Cancer, Abortion and Abortifacients

The month of October is often the month dedicated to breast cancer awareness. Many television networks, such as Lifetime Television, and many other network programs place great emphasis on informing the public about the causes, treatments, and the importance of early detection.

What is astonishing is that one never hears on the networks and very rarely in the print media the scientifically well-established and well-known correlation between breast cancer and abortion (and one could even say hormonal contraceptives that serve as abortifacients).

Why is this so? What are so many people afraid of?

Breast cancer is the leading cause of cancer death in the United States for women between the ages of 29–59. Every year, approximately 180,000 women are diagnosed with breast cancer and more than 41,000 die from this disease. One out of every eight women will develop breast cancer during their lifetime (CDC, 2000).

Over the past forty-three years twenty-seven out of thirty-three worldwide studies have shown a correlation between breast cancer and abortion. In the United States, thirteen out of fourteen studies of American women have implicated abortion as a risk factor for breast cancer. The United Kingdom's Royal College of Obstetricians and Gynecologists advices physicians who perform abortions to inform their patients of the risk factor between abortion and breast cancer (RCOG, 2000). In a 1995 Harvard University study of over 2,000 women in Greece, the study found that women who had abortions had a fifty-one percent higher rate of breast cancer (*Int., J. Cancer*, Vol. 61). It has also been cited that women under thirty who have had an abortion and have a family history of breast cancer increase their risk of breast cancer by eighty percent. After the age of thirty, this increases to 270 percent. Women with a family history of breast cancer and who have had two or more abortions have a 600 percent increased risk of developing breast cancer.

Women younger than eighteen who have had an abortion have a 150 percent increased risk of developing breast cancer, with an 800 percent increased risk if they had their abortions between the ninth and twenty-fourth week of pregnancy (cf. *Clincial Oncology*, 1989, 1:11-18; *Am. J. Epidemiol*, 1990, 131:804-814; *Brit. Med. J.* 1990, 299:1430-1432; *Cancer* 1991, 67:1285-1290; *Int. J. Cancer*, 1991, 48:816-820; *JNCI*, 1994, 86:1584-1592; *J. Epidemiol*, 1996, 50:481-496).

The biological hypothesis for the correlation between abortion and breast cancer is still uncertain, but the American Cancer Society in 1997 proposed the following theory—oddly a theory they would eliminate from their website after 1997. Could it be that the pro-abortion forces had any influence on them? In any event, in 1997 they argued the following: "Breast cells have been hypothesized to be the most susceptible to transformation into malignant cells when breast tissue contains primarily rapidly growing and undifferentiated epithelial cells—i.e., during adolescence and pregnancy. Some investigators have hypothesized that the termination of pregnancy in the first two trimesters may alter the carcinogenic potential of breast tissue by interrupting the complete differentiation of breast cells that occurs during full-term pregnancy and confers protection." Dr. Chris Kahlenborn, the author of "Breast Cancer Risk and Abortion," explains it in a simpler manner: "At the beginning of pregnancy there are great increases in certain hormone levels (i.e., estrogen, progesterone, etc.) that support pregnancy. In response to these changes breast cells divide and mature into cells able to produce milk. Abortion causes an abrupt fall in hormone levels, leaving breast cells in an immature state. These immature cells can more easily become cancer cells."

Putting an end to abortion would eliminate the No. 1 preventable risk of breast cancer (*Chicago Tribune*, May 21, 2001).

What can be said of abortion can be said of those contraceptives that act as abortificients—abortion causing agents. Is it is a coincidence that one of the side effects associated with oral contraceptives include the development of breast lumps? Is it a coincidence that those who have a family history of breast cancer are warned to avoid oral contraceptives (cf. PDR, 2000)?

Let us break the silence. Let us make what is well known to scientists in the field of breast cancer research well known to all. Let us proclaim what twenty-seven out of thirty-three studies have shown over forty-three years. Let us show the world who truly loves women.

10

Adoption, the Loving Choice

As long as I live I will always remember a debate that took place in my religion class when I was a Catholic schoolteacher.

The debate was over the issue of abortion. It is sad to say that although this was a Catholic school, the class was divided over the issue. Many children had been indoctrinated into the culture of death's pro-abortion stance.

I will always remember one particular boy who led the pro-abortionists in the debate. He knew every cliché and every pro-abortion argument. His father was a writer for a local daily newspaper (renowned for its anti-Catholic stands) and a pro-abortionist. The boy had learned well from his father.

The debate went back and forth for close to forty-minutes. Every possible argument on both sides of the issue had been exhausted.

At this point I made the decision to stop the debate and move on to another subject. I knew that no consensus could be found amongst students.

The class was divided into two irreconcilable visions of reality, two irreconcilable worldviews.

The culture of death and the culture of life had come face to face.

Just when I had given up all hope, the shiest little girl in the class raised her hand. This surprised me as well as all the students.

This little girl rarely spoke up in class, yet she always attracted much attention.

The girls all wanted to be her friend and the boys all wanted to impress her. So when this girl raised her hand, the entire class was completely focused on hearing what she had to say.

I will never forget her words. She said: "When my mom was pregnant she was going to have an abortion, but she decided to put me up for adoption instead. I'm so glad she did. I have the best adoptive parents in the world. I love my parents so much and I love my life. I'm so happy I'm alive. I'm so happy I was adopted."

In all my years as a schoolteacher I never heard a class become so quiet.

A pin could have dropped and the whole class would have heard it hit the ground. The debate had been won. Christ had prevailed.

Several months ago I was having my car repaired at a local dealership when this girl, now a college educated, well-adjusted, joyful adult, came into the dealership hand in hand with her father.

Her smile brightened the entire room. What a wonderful gift she had become to the world, I thought.

According to U.S. Health and Human Services, the average abortion takes five to ten minutes to perform, while the average wait to adopt a child is two to ten years.

Instead of aborting one out of every four children in this country, we should be saving these children in order to provide childless parents with children.

Instead of abortion, the loving choice of adoption should be the option for mothers who are unwilling or incapable of being adequate parents.

Let us not extinguish pretty smiles.

11

Never-Ending Hope

A professor of philosophy asked his students to debate an issue. The professor stated: "What would you do given the following situation?"

There was a man who was born into a poor family where his distant alcoholic father would beat him on a nightly basis. He lived in a hostile and abusive home environment.

In adulthood, he suffered from bouts of depression, irritability, and various mental and panic disorders. He suffered from bouts of chronic abdominal pain and colic, diarrhea, nausea, thoracic gout, plumbism, poor digestion, rheumaticism, deafness, alcoholism and possibly syphilis.

He was a complete failure in love and in his relationships.

Given what you know, would it have been better for this person to never have been born?

The overwhelming answer came back, "Yes. No one should be asked to live such a life," the students answered.

The professor stared at the students and quietly responded: "You have just killed Beethoven!"

The class was silenced.

How many Beethoven's have we killed? How many Pius Xs, John Paul IIs, Martin Luther Kings, Gandhis, Mother Teresas of Calcutta, George Washingtons, Abraham Lincolns, Michelangelos, Raphaels, Shakespeares, Dantes, and so forth, have been aborted? How many religious leaders, presidents, world leaders, discoverers, scientists, doctors, teachers have been aborted?

Would there still be cancer in the world? Would there still be heart disease? What about diabetes, Parkinson's, Alzheimer's, schizophrenia, depression, pneumonia, influenza, cerebral palsy, hepatitis, HIV, AIDS, kidney and liver decease? Have we killed the person or persons who would have cured these diseases?

12

Pro-life Street Activity: What would Jesus do?

"What would Jesus do?" This is a question that pro-life individuals often ask themselves when seeking the prudent approach to changing pro-abortion hearts into pro-life hearts.

Yet this question is not as easy to answer as one would think.

For some the most effective method of changing hearts and putting an end to abortion is by resorting to the power of the Mass, the Rosary, and the intercessory power of Our Lady of Guadalupe and all the saints. These individuals believe that prayer, respect and obedience to the law are the most effective means of combating the evil forces that envelop the killing of innocent life.

Others, building upon the foundation of prayer, are firm believers in civil disobedience in the tradition of Martin Luther King Jr. Many people, such as the renowned Father Benedict Groeschel, believe that abortion is such an egregious assault on God's gift of life that one must be willing to bear the cross of Jesus Christ and to imitate him in calling for repentance and reform, even to the point of arrest.

Marches and life chains are other methods of combating abortion. Whether one walks through cities or neighborhoods or whether one stands side by side on a sidewalk, the object is to make people confront what they often don't want to confront, the evil of abortion. These groups have signs that read, "Abortion kills Children," "Abortion is Racist," Adoption, the Loving Option," "Jesus Forgives and Heals," and "Abortion Hurts Women." They often carry enlarged graphic pictures of aborted children. In recent years, they have resorted to pro-life floats, motorcades, and even trucks with large depictions of aborted children. In recent times, the first television broadcast of aborted children was shown on the Catholic television network, EWTN.

Some psychologists such as Theresa Burke, the founder of Rachel's Vineyard, a healing program for women who have had abortions, feel that graphic pictures can be detrimental to the healing process of women suffering from post-abortion trauma. Others, however, argue that the graphic pictures help to awaken an awareness of repressed post-abortion trauma in women's lives, and therefore direct them on the road to seeking help and healing. They point to the statistical reality that men and women who are vehemently hostile to graphic pictures of aborted children are often men and women who have repressed their participation in abortion during some time in their lives. Furthermore, many post abortive women feel that if only someone had been there to show them the evil that abortion produces in such a graphic manner, they would have never gone through with their abortion.

Another objection is that small children should not be exposed to such graphic, brutal pictures. The answer given to this objection is that the reality that is modern life is engulfed with graphic pictures. They are found all around us, on billboards, in television commercials, on newscasts, in movies, comics, cartoons, on magazine and newspaper covers, in toys and games, and so forth. Charitable organizations display pictures of deformed children in wheelchairs. They display graphic pictures of the poor, the hungry, the orphans, and the marginalized in the worst of conditions in effort to move hearts to help.

We pray the Stations of the Cross where graphic pictures are shown of Jesus being condemned, falling, stripped of clothing, nailed to a cross, dying and laid in a tomb. We pray the Rosary where one meditates, no matter the age, on the agony in the garden, the scourging at the pillar, the crowning with thorns, the carrying of the cross, and the crucifixion.

And what about the Bible? The Bible is fixed with graphic, horrifying imagery. Remember John the Baptist and his head.

Those who favor graphic images of aborted children often point to Jesus' and Mother Teresa of Calcutta's reaction to graphic images. Did Jesus look away from the leper's face, arms, hands, legs, and eyes? Did Mother Teresa turn away from a seventy pound dying man being eaten up by maggots?

The supporters of graphic pictures of murdered human beings point out that Jesus was the ultimate graphic image and therefore the ultimate image for the pro-life movement.

Jesus was scourged at the pillar. The unborn child's body is ravaged by being sucked and ripped apart by a suction catheter.

Jesus was pierced in the arms and legs with nails. An unborn child has his hands and legs torn apart.

Jesus was crowned with thorns. An unborn child's head is opened by a Metzenbaum scissor where the contents of the head are emptied and the skull is crushed.

Jesus was offered a drink from a sponge. An unborn child is given a saline solution that is swallowed causing salt poisoning, dehydration, hemorrhaging, convulsions and death.

Jesus was pierced with a lance and blood and fluid came out. Through a procedure called intercardiac injection, a fluid-filled needle pierces the heart of the unborn child and causes death.

What we do to these unborn children we do to Jesus. The blood of these infants is the blood of Christ.

We are a culture filled with graphic and anti-Christian images. Just as a mother monitors what her child sees, she can likewise monitor the viewing of aborted children. These pictures don't pop out of nowhere. A picket line is seen from great distances, up to a mile, and so one has plenty of time to say, "Turn your head or close your eyes." You have more time to have your child turn away from a picket line than you do in having your child turn away from the ever present moral debauchery that is inflicted upon your child's eyes and mind on television!

Many argue it is better to hurt some feelings, than to allow the indifference over the issue of abortion to continue, particularly in the Christian community. It is hurt feelings over the pictures of lynched African-Americans that began changing attitudes. It is the hideous graphic images of underage working children that hurt many feelings and led to child labor laws. It is hurt feelings over the carnage of the Vietnam War that put an end to it. It is the hurt feelings from the graphic images of the World Trade Center building imploding that led to a war on terrorism and the war in Iraq. Afflicted feelings cause change. They didn't persecute and kill the prophets for being politically correct.

The lax approach to combating abortion and the indifference that pervades much of modern society has led many to seek out more challenging approaches. In recent times, there has been a movement focusing on picketing churches with "love life expositions." The Palm Beach County Right to Life League has been taking this approach for years. Many argue that this approach does more harm than good in that it tends to divide the pro-life community, and a community divided is a community bound to fail. However, those who favor picketing churches are quick to point out that pastors, priests, ministers, and lay persons are often more interested in being "country club administrators and parishioners" where one is not challenged to grow, where the Gospel of the cross is never taught. They point out that bishops have failed miserably in their leadership as shepherds. They say: "I guarantee that if bishops began excommunicating Catholics who took pro-abortion stances, the country would be radically changed." They point out that approximately fifty percent of Catholics vote pro-choice, a vote that assures the continuation of legalized abortion. How can this be after thirty years, if the clergy is doing its work? They argue that politicians calling themselves Catholic constantly take pro-abortion, pro culture of death positions. They argue that the reason the South never became Catholic was in part due to the fact that many Catholic clergymen failed to stand up against slavery out of the fear of hurting the feelings of their slave-owning parishioners. They point out the failure of the German clergy in adequately opposing Nazism and the killing of millions of Jews, all out of a fear of hurting the feelings of parishioners. Hurt feelings cannot be compared to an aborted, torn-up, disfigured child.

Within the boundaries of each parish in the diocese of Miami there are over 7 abortions in a week per parish boundary. In terms of all other deaths within one week in a parish boundary there are 6 deaths. The abortionists in Miami are busier than the undertakers (cf. Geisman, Palm Beach County Right to Life League, 2003). Where are our bishops? Paper on ink just doesn't do to satisfy the cause of life!

Whatever one's view is on the issue, the approach that uses imagery has had success. It is not unusual to see women stopping their cars along the side of the street, pull down their windows, and say, "Keep up the good work. If it wasn't for these pictures, I would have had an abortion, but now I have the most precious gift of all, a precious daughter. Thank you. Thank you."

Somewhat related to the above approach is a method of protest that focuses on picketing specific institutions or public figures. Pro-lifers will use signs and pictures to target a specific institution or public figure that provides or supports abortion. Abortion facilities, hospitals, homes, offices, and so forth, are picketed.

Doctor's homes and offices have been picketed with signs saying, "Do you know that your neighbor is an abortionist?" Do you know your doctor is an abortionist?" This approach is responsible for—perhaps more than any other method—the shortage of abortionists in this country.

Sidewalk counseling is a pro-life activity which focuses on offering women, in a gentle and respectful manner, alternatives to abortions. Women, as they approach the abortion facility, are told where the local pregnancy center can be found and are promised the support of the Church. Karen Black, a well-known Atlanta sidewalk counselor, has been credited with over 1,000 "turnarounds," that is, people who decided to keep their child.

Education of the public is also another form of promoting life. The distribution of pro-life fliers and the practice of what Fr. Frank Pavone calls, "teach-ins" is also a method of educating the public. In Father Pavone's words, "in a teach-in a handful of pro-lifers gather on a street corner or other public area and begin speaking aloud on the abortion issue" (*Our Media is the Streets*, 11).

After all that has been said, the question still remains: "What would Jesus do?" As one can see, the answer to that question is not so easy to answer. In fact, it has been one of the most difficult questions that to this day I struggle with."

At this point in my spiritual journey I favor the approach of the Helpers of God's Precious Infants (although I must admit that as I get older I feel a tendency toward more aggressive approaches). This approach emphasizes the power of the Mass, the Rosary at the abortion facility, Benediction, sidewalk counseling, and the intercessory power of the saints, particularly Our Lady of Guadalupe. No signs or pictures are present during prayer sessions. (However, signs and graphic pictures are appropriate in non-prayer settings). The Helpers of God's Precious Infants believe that prayer, respect, and obedience to the law are the most effective means of combating the evil forces that envelop the killing of innocent life.

Another area I favor promoting and bringing to the forefront is the reality of post-abortion trauma. I am firmly convinced that the women who have been healed or are still suffering from post-abortion trauma will be the ones responsible for putting an end to abortion. They are the secondary silent victims that will awaken to shake the world! One can turn one's eyes from a picture of an aborted child, but one cannot turn away from a woman that faces you with the scars of abortion.

While I favor a particular approach, I in no way oppose the other methods mentioned above for they are all part of acceptable Catholic practices since they are all non-violent in approach.

Ultimately one must follow one's informed conscience guided by prudence. And whether one agrees or disagrees with a particular approach, one must respect the conscience of others.

13

Embryonic Stem Cell Research: Hindering Moral Scientific Advancement

Stem cells are cells that have not undergone maturation and theoretically can become any of the 220 cell types and any of the 210 specialized tissue types that make up the human body.

Because stem cells are like "blank slates," they theoretically can morph into any kind of human tissue. They theoretically can become replacement parts for unhealthy cells and tissues. The benefits from stem cell research provides the future with great possibilities in the cure and treatment of illnesses, such as Parkinson's, Alzheimer's, heart disease, and diabetes.

Stem cells can be obtained immorally by the destruction of human life (i.e., human embryos) or they can be obtained morally from adults in a safe manner (i.e., from muscles, umbilical cords, bone marrow, the placenta, and from a wide variety of other adult tissues). The media and Hollywood stars, such as Mary Tyler Moore and Christopher Reeve, have embraced embryonic stem research with a passion.

What is even more outrageous is that seventy percent of Catholics support embryonic stem cell research (*Newsweek*, July 9, 2001). Yet the reality is that embryonic stem cells have never helped a human patient (NCCB, Life Issue Forum, 2001; *Science*, April, 2001).

During the National Academy of Sciences' workshop on "Stem Cells and the Future of Regenerative Medicine" held in Washington, D.C., Marcus Grompe, M.D., Ph.D., an expert in molecular and medical genetics, stated: "There is no evidence of therapeutic benefit from embryonic stem cells," and Dr. Bert Vogelstein, chairman of John Hopkins University's Institute of Medicine studying stem cell research pointed out that any therapeutic claim of benefit from embryonic stem cell research is purely "conjectural."

On the other hand, great success has been attained in the use of adult stem cells. Adult stem cells not only have a future in curing and treating illnesses, they are doing so right now. Adult stem cells are currently being used in the treatment of multiple sclerosis, lupus, rheumatoid arthritis, stroke, anemia, Epstein-Barr virus infection, cornea damage, blood and liver diseases, brain tumors, retinoblastoma, ovarian cancer, solid tumors, testicular cancer, leukemia, breast cancer, neuroblastoma, non-Hodgkins' lymphoma, renal cell carcinoma, diabetes, heart damage; as well as cartilage, bone, muscle, and spinal-cord damage (NCCB, Life Issue Forum, 2001; *Science*, April, 2001; *Lancet*, January 2001; *APR*, 2000).

Given the benefits of adult stem cells, the question must be asked: Why are so many individuals preoccupied with embryonic stem cell research which involves the destruction of human life? Given the success of adult stem cells, you would think that these individuals would want improved funding and research in the field of adult stem cell experimentation.

The media and Hollywood's preoccupation with embryonic stem cells is an assault on the dignity of human life and a hindrance to the advancement of sound, moral science.

And even if one day it can be shown that embryonic stem cell research is beneficial for many, it cannot be an acceptable practice. One does not improve one's standard of life over the death of another!

His Holiness Pope John Paul II suffers from Parkinson's, and I don't see him crying out for embryonic stem cell research. Quite the contrary.

14

Human Cloning: Playing God

"We are going to be one with God. We are going to have almost as much knowledge and almost as much power as God" (Richard Sheed, National Public Radio, 98).

In theory, human cloning is a way of producing a genetic replica of a person without sexual reproduction.

Cloning occurs when the nuclear material from a cell of an organism's body (a somatic cell) is transplanted into a female reproductive cell (an oocyte) whose nuclear material has been removed or inactivated in order to produce a new, genetically identical organism.

Those who favor cloning argue that one could theoretically harvest cells, blood, tissues, and much needed organs such as hearts, livers and kidneys for therapeutic use.

These harvested "products" would be considered ideal for they would be immunologically matched—that is, they would eliminate the need for life-long immunosuppressive therapy (Ahmann, NCBQ, 2001).

At another level, cloning would provide a means for sterile couples to reproduce.

At a glance cloning may appear appealing to some but in reality it is radically evil. As the ethicist Hans Jonas has written, [human cloning] is the most despotic...and the most slavish form of genetic manipulation" (*Tecnica, medicina edetica*, 1997).

The *Pontificia Academia Pro Vita* in its "Reflections on Cloning" points out that human cloning would radically damage the meaning, rationality, and complimentarity of human reproduction:

- The unitive, bonding aspect of human sexual reproduction would be lost in cloning. The precious gift of sexual intercourse as a physical and spiritual act between a man and a woman would become non-existent. A woman in theory could take the nuclear material from a somatic cell from her body and fuse it into her own ovum and produce a genetic reproduction of herself without any need of a husband.

- The naturally occurring balance between the male and female sex in society as well as the natural structure of the family would inevitably become distorted. As the document "Reflections on Cloning" explains: It is conceivable that "a woman could [end up being] the twin sister of her mother, lack a biological father and be the daughter of her grandfather."

- Human life would become viewed more as a "product," an object to be harvested, rather than as a gift of love. Cloning would suppress personal identity and subjectivity at the cost of biological qualities that could be appraised and selected. Women would be exploited for their ova and their wombs, being seen simply in terms of their "purely biological functions."

- Cloning could lead to a loss of genetic variation in society, thereby making society vulnerable to catastrophic illnesses and genetic defects. Naturally occurring mutations would not be sufficient to assure genetic variation.

- Cloning would lead to a wide array of psychological problems, whereby one would be troubled by questions such as: Who is my father? Who is my mother? Do I even have a father and mother? Who am I? What am I? Where do I come from?

- Cloning could lead to even greater trauma in the lives of parents who have lost a beloved child. The assumption from some heartbroken parents would be that if they could only clone their dead child, they would somehow have him or her back again. But this is not the case. A cloned individual would have a different soul and a different cultural and environmental upbringing. This child would not be what they desired or intended.

- One's "quality of life" would become a surrogate for one's search for meaning and salvation. A culture that is already self-centered, and selfish would become even more so. It would become even more an "I, me, mine" culture.

- Human cloning could be the ultimate expression of narcissism and hedonism. One could envision a world that desires to clone only the so-called "beautiful" people. And who determines who are the beautiful people? In

God's eyes we are all beautiful. Furthermore, one could envision a society in which a self-absorbed person would clone himself or herself so as to have spare parts in the event of illnesses.

- And finally, but most importantly, cloning would assault the dignity of human life in the most cruel and exploitative way imaginable by making cloned children the subject of experiments and by preventing their births. Dr. Ian Wilmut was only capable of producing Dolly, the cloned sheep, after 277 attempts at cloning. In terms of human beings no culture could morally sustain itself by killing 277 human embryos with the hope of one surviving, nor allow for the current rate of 95 to 99 percent of embryos to die in the process of cloning.

Richard Sheed's words echo ominously: "We are going to become one with God. We are going to have almost as much knowledge and almost as much power as God." Cloning is an experiment in playing God. And we all know what happened in the story of Adam and Eve when they attempted to play God.

Let us not make the same mistake. Let us not participate in the downfall of Western civilization.

15

Genetic Engineering, Assisted Reproduction, Scientific Research

Scientific and medical experiments on human individuals can have great benefits for the healing of the sick. However, any forms of experimentation or science which conflicts with the dignity of the human person and the moral law are to be prohibited.

As the Catechism of the Catholic Church states:

"Basic scientific research, as well as applied research, is a significant expression of man's dominion over creation. Science and technology are precious resources when placed at the service of man and promote his integral development for the benefit of all. By themselves however they cannot disclose the meaning of existence and of human progress. Science and technology are ordered to man, from whom they take their origin and development; hence they find in the person and in his moral values both evidence of their purpose and awareness of their limits (2293)."

"It is an illusion to claim moral neutrality in scientific research and its applications. On the other hand, guiding principles cannot be inferred from simple technical efficiency, or from the usefulness accruing to some at the expense of others or, even worse, from prevailing ideologies. Science and technology by their very nature require unconditional respect for fundamental moral criteria. They must be at the service of the human person, of his inalienable rights, of his true and integral good, in conformity with the plan and the will of God (CCC 2294)."

Organ Transplants and Donations

Organ transplants are accepted as long as they conform to the moral law; that is, as long as "the physical and psychological dangers and risks to the donor are proportionate to the good that is sought for the recipient" CCC 2296).

Organ donation after death is a holy, noble, and meritorious act of love and solidarity with one's fellow human being, and is in no way contrary to the moral law.

One cannot resort, however, to the disabling mutilation of the body or the death of a human person in order to obtain an organ or organs.

At the heart of organ transplants and donations is the requirement of consent. If the donor's organ or organs are removed without his or her consent, or the consent of a legitimate proxy, then the removal of any organ or organs is an infringement on the dignity of the human body.

Autopsies

Autopsies are permitted for legal inquests and the good of scientific research as long as the body is treated with respect and charity.

Artificial Insemination

Scientific research that aims at eliminating or overcoming sterility is of great merit as long as it seeks to maintain the unitive and procreative dimensions of the sexual act.

It is gravely immoral to separate a husband from his wife (and vice versa) by introducing a third person into the reproductive process.

Donum Vitae II, 1, 5, 4 states:

"Techniques that entail the dissociation of husband and wife, by the intrusion of a person other than the couple (donation of sperm, or ovum, surrogate uterus), are gravely immoral. These techniques (heterologous artificial insemination and fertilization) infringe the child's right to be born of a father and mother known to him and bound to each other by marriage. They betray the spouses' right to become a father and a mother only through each other."

"Techniques involving only the married couple (homologous artificial insemination and fertilization) are perhaps less reprehensible, yet remain morally unacceptable. They dissociate the sexual act from the procreative act. The act which brings the child into existence is no longer an act by which two persons give themselves to one another, but one that 'entrusts the life and identity of the embryo into the power of doctors and biologists and establishes the domination of technology over the origin and destiny of the human person. Such a relationship of domination is in itself contrary to the dignity and equality that must be common to parents and children.' Under the moral aspect procreation is deprived of its proper perfection when it is not willed as the fruit of the conjugal act, that is to say, of the specific act of the spouses' union…Only respect for the link between the meanings of the conjugal act and respect for the unity of the human being make possible procreation in conformity with the dignity of the person,"

At the heart of Catholic sexuality is the inseparable bond between the unitive and procreative dimensions of the conjugal act.

These teachings can be a tremendous cross upon a couple that so much desires the gift of children. It must be remembered that children are gifts from God; they are not property that is owed to a couple. No one has a "right to a child." Only the child has rights, the right "to be the fruit of the specific act of the conjugal love of his parents," and "the right to be respected as a person from the moment of conception" (cf. CCC 2378; CDF, *Donum Vitae* II, 8).

For those who are unable to have children by moral means, they are encouraged to unite themselves to the sufferings of Christ, to become generative by their works of charity, and to seek the alternative of adoption, the giving a loving home for parentless children, children hungering for the love of parents.

Designer Babies

When one is able to clone or to select what sex, hair or eye color, intellect, body structure, and so forth by genetic engineering and the manipulation and choice of embryos one is going down a dangerous path. Huge distortions in the gene pool—which is essential for a healthy population—and huge distortions in the balance of the sexes in the population are bound to occur—cultures that prefer male children (often poor countries) will be overpopulated with males and cultures that favor female children will lead to an overpopulation in females. Designer babies will lead to distorted populations susceptible to grave illnesses, because of the diminished gene pool and the imbalance of the sexes.

The striking, unique and unrepeatable qualities that make each of us special and distinctively beautiful are at stake when a culture seeks to play God. A culture that flirts with manipulating the origins of life, is a culture flirting with extinction.

"Certain attempts to influence chromosomic or genetic inheritance are not therapeutic but are aimed at producing human beings selected according to sex or other predetermined qualities. Such manipulations are contrary to the personal dignity of the human being and his integrity and identity which are unique and unrepeatable" (Donum Vitae I, 6).

Prenatal Diagnosis

Prenatal diagnosis can be used as a tool for protecting the integrity of an unborn child. It provides physicians with the ability to take care for and heal unborn children, even by means of performing surgical procedures within a mother's womb. As *Donum Vitae* I, 2 indicates:

Prenatal diagnosis is morally licit, "if it respects the life and integrity of the embryo and the human fetus and is directed toward its safeguarding or healing as an individual...It is gravely opposed to the moral law when this is done with the thought of possibly inducing an abortion, depending upon the results: a diagnosis must not be the equivalent of a death sentence."

Prenatal Surgery

Prenatal surgery is a powerful gift as long as the surgery is directed toward the healing and care of the child and does not involve disproportionate risks.

"One must hold as licit procedures carried out on the human embryo which respect the life and integrity of the embryo and do not involve disproportionate risks for it, but are directed toward its healing, the improvement of its condition of health, or its individual survival" (Donum Vitae, I, 3).

An Often Overlooked Reality of Cloning, Embryonic Stem Cell Research, and Invitro-Fertilization

One of the often overlooked evils associated with the above practices is that in the process of cloning, or doing embryonic stem cell research, or attempting to have a child by means of artificial insemination, embryos are exploited and killed during the process—often in astronomical proportions. And it is for this reason the Church states that "it is immoral to produce human embryos intended for exploitation and as disposable biological material" (*Donum Vitae* I, 5).

Failure to respect the dignity of the human person from conception to natural death ultimately leads to the disintegration and death of a culture. And sadly to say, we are living in a time when Western civilization is beginning its downfall.

16

Euthanasia Versus Palliative Care

"I have had lots of patients who wanted to commit suicide, but you don't help them do it. You learn why patients don't want to live anymore. If they're in pain, you give them more or better medication. If they have trouble with their families, you help them get the problem solved."

—*Elizabeth Kubler-Ross*

Elizabeth Kubler-Ross was a world-renowned medical doctor and psychiatrist. She did much research and wrote several books and articles in the area of death and dying. In her research, she found that people who face death often experience episodes of denial, anger, bargaining with God, and depression. Most importantly, she pointed out that if a patient was lovingly cared for, the patient's last moments would be ones filled with acceptance and even hope.

Direct euthanasia consists in the murdering of the handicapped, the ill, and the dying—with or without their consent and knowledge—and is thus morally unacceptable (CCC 2277). In the definition used by the Congregation for the Doctrine of the Faith in its *Declaration on Euthanasia* we read: "By euthanasia is understood an action or omission of an action which of itself or by intention causes death in order that all suffering may be eliminated" (CDF, 1980a). And in *Evangelium Vitae* we read from the Holy Father that "Euthanasia is a violation of the law of God, since it is the deliberate and morally unacceptable killing of a person" (n. 65).

Today, too many terminally ill patients are being euthanized before they have come to a stage of acceptance and peace. Too many people are being put to death in times of anger, loneliness, and depression. A great injustice is being done to such people, all in the name of compassion.

The Church in its respect for the dignity of human life, and in its respect for God as the living Creator, promotes a holy death, a holy "letting go" which is filled with acceptance, peace, and hope on the part of the person entering into eternity.

The Church supports palliative care; that is, a form of care which seeks to eliminate pain and understands the redemptive value of unavoidable suffering (CCC 2279; cf. Col. 1:24). The Church therefore strongly encourages the use of painkillers in alleviating suffering, for at no stage is the "ordinary care owed to a sick person…[to be] interrupted" (CCC 2279). And for whatever pain remains, the Church encourages one to unite that suffering with Christ's for the good of one's soul and the souls of those in purgatory.

My uncle died at the young age of fifty-eight from terminal cancer. He received the best of palliative care. He died a peaceful, joyous and holy death in the arms of his loving family. Let no one deprive us of this!

17

Letting Go, Discontinuing Medical Procedures

Prolonging life at all cost has never been part of the Catholic tradition (NCCB, 1986). There are times when one must let go and allow oneself or a loved one to enter into eternity.

In the Congregation for the Doctrine of the Faith's document *Donum Vitae* we read: "Discontinuing medical procedures that are burdensome, dangerous, extraordinary, or disproportionate to the expected outcome can be legitimate; it is the refusal of "over-zealous" treatment. Here one does not will to cause death (as in the case of euthanasia); one's inability to impede it is merely accepted."

Pope John Paul II in *Evangelium Vitae* writes: "When death is clearly imminent and inevitable, one can in conscience refuse forms of treatment that would only secure a precarious and burdensome prolongation of life, so long as the normal care of the sick person in similar cases is not interrupted" (CCC 2278).

The normal care of the person consists of prolonging life by ordinary means as opposed to extraordinary means. To put it more succinctly, the ordinary and obligatory means of prolonging life involve "all medicines, treatments, and operations which offer a reasonable hope of benefit for the patient and which can be obtained or used without excessive expense, pain, or burden" (Pius XII, Discourse on Doctors, 1957).

This is often understood to mean that proper nutrition (including intravenous feeding) and hydration are not to be withheld as long as sufficient benefit can be obtained. In the U.S. National Conference of Bishops' *Ethical and Religious Directives*, directive 58 explains: "There should be a presumption in favor of providing nutrition and hydration to all patients, including patients who require

46

medically assisted nutrition and hydration, as long as this is of sufficient benefit to outweigh the burdens involved to the patient."

In terms of those means of treatment which can be discontinued, Pius XII argues: "All medicines, treatments, and operations, which cannot be used or obtained without excessive expense, pain, or other burden [can be refused]." In other terms, when therapy will not benefit the person, "letting go" is ethically justifiable. To disconnect a respirator when a person has reached the point of no return is ethically acceptable and appropriate.

The decision to let go is ideally made in an environment where the doctor, the priest, and the family come together to pray and say, "We are here for you." It is a time where one prepares the person for eternity through the sacrament of the sick and if possible viaticum, the Eucharist for the journey. It is a time when one is aware that life never truly ends, but only changes. It is the recognition that just as a person loved you and prayed for you on his or her earthly journey, he or she will be loving you and praying for you in the presence of almighty God. "Letting go" is not the end, but the beginning of a new phase of eternal life.

18

Homosexual Activity, A Pro-life Issue

Many might be tempted to say, "What in the world does homosexual activity have to do with the Pro-life movement and the "culture of life?" The answer is quite simple. When the sanctity of the sexual act is lost, then the structure of the family and society is doomed.

As a Christian and as a priest I never thought that a teaching that has existed from the beginning of Christianity to the twentieth century would ever be questioned.

But to my horror and sadness, in recent years many openly and actively practicing homosexuals have been ordained to the ministry of various protestant denominations. How can this be?

The Catholic Church basing "itself on Sacred Scripture, which presents homosexual acts as acts of grave depravity, [and] tradition has always declared that homosexual acts are intrinsically disordered" (CCC 2357; CDF, *Persona Humana*, 8). "They are contrary to the natural law. They close the sexual act to the gift of life. They do not proceed from genuine affective and sexual complementarity. Under no circumstances can they be approved" (CCC 2357).

Scripture is clear. The story of Sodom and Gomorrah in Genesis 19:1-14, while often argued as an account of inhospitality, is an account of the evil of homosexual activity; otherwise, why would all generations call those who perform homosexual acts sodomites? Furthermore, can you ever give an account of God destroying an entire city with fire and brimstone for simply failing to be hospitable?

Leviticus 18:22 states: "You shall not lie with a man as with a woman; such a thing is an abomination."

Now some like to argue that there are many things forbidden by the Hebrew Scriptures which are no longer held by Christians. There are those laws which Jesus specifically addressed as in the case of what to do with those caught in adultery (Jn. 8:3f) or in the case of those suffering from leprosy (Lk. 5:13). And there is the example of eliminating the laws of circumcisions by the Apostles empowered by Christ and the Spirit (Acts 15). And there is the making of all that was once "unclean" clean in Peter's revelation (Acts 10:9-33).

The point is that unless Jesus and his Church specifically clarified and overturned certain Hebraic laws, the laws were to remain. Leviticus forbids sex with your mother (18:7), with your sister (18:9), and with your aunt (18:14). It forbids bestiality (18:23) and orgies (18:23). I guess those who do not like the Hebraic laws are in favor of practicing these evils?

But let us look at the New Testament writings written after the death and resurrection of Christ, when the Spirit of truth (Jn. 15:26; 16:13) was to be sent to the Christian community. Furthermore, let us never forget the promises of Christ, the promise that the gates of hell would not prevail against his Church (Mt. 16:18f; Jn. 16:13; 28:20; 1 Tim. 3:15) and the promise that he would be with his Church till the end of time (Jn. 20:29).

Let us remember that the letters to Timothy, the Romans, and to the Corinthians in the Bible were written by Christ's greatest theologian, Paul, who lived after the resurrection of Jesus! If it wasn't for Paul, we would know very little about Christ, his Church, and Christianity in general!

In 1 Corinthians 6:9-10 we read: "Do not be deceived; neither fornicators or idolaters nor adulterers nor boy prostitutes nor sodomites…will inherit the kingdom of God."

In Romans 1:26-27 the Scriptures declare: Their females exchanged natural relations for unnatural, and the males likewise gave up natural relations with females and burn with lust for one another. Males did shameful things with males and thus received in their own persons the due penalty for their perversity."

In 1 Timothy 1:10-11 we read: The "law is meant not for a righteous person but for the lawless and unruly, the godless and sinful, the unholy and profane, those who killed their fathers and mothers, murderers, the unchaste, sodomites, kidnappers, liars, perjurers, and whatever else is opposed to sound teaching, according to the glorious gospel of the blessed God, with which I have been entrusted."

But it is not simply individual quotes that condemn homosexual acts, the very theology of the Old and New Testaments condemn it. The underlying theology of God's love for his people in the Old and New Testament is based on the complementarity of the sexes and on the natural law which underlies this complimentarity. Men and women are physically and psychologically different, and it is in this distinction that the complementarity between a man and a woman make the possibility of two becoming one (cf. Mt. 19:3-6; Mk. 10:6-9). The theology of Genesis and the entire Pentateuch, the theology of the Wisdom and Prophetic books of the Bible are all based on the underlying theology of the love of God for his people in the form of the love of a man for a woman in their distinct natures. In fact, there is *no way* of understanding the Scriptures without understanding the relationship between the sexes!

Tradition is clear. Some sixteen century before the birth of most Protestant denominations, Christians believed that homosexual acts were contrary to the will of God.

In the *Didache, The Teaching of the Twelve Apostles*, written anywhere from 65 AD to 120 AD we are told to "not be sexually perverted by committing sodomy" (cf. 4). In Polycarp's *Letter to the Philippians*, the disciple of the apostle John states: "Sodomites shall not inherit the Kingdom of God." And in Barnabas, often attributed as the same Barnabas who was the companion of Paul, we read: "Thou shall not commit sodomy" (n. 19).

Other Fathers of the Church who have condemned homosexual acts include the following Apostolic Fathers—those who knew the apostles: Clement of Rome (ca. 88-97), a friend of the apostles Peter and Paul and ordained by them; Ignatius of Antioch (martyred in 107), a convert of the apostle John and consecrated bishop of Antioch by the apostle Peter and Paul; Papias (ca. 67-140), disciple of Polycarp and an "acquaintance of the apostles"; Hermas (ca. d. 155) of Romans 16:14.

In terms of the post-apostolic Fathers the following condemned homosexual acts: Caius, Presbyter of Rome (ca. 198); Dionysius of Corinth (ca. 166); Quadratus (ca. 125); Aristedes of Athens (ca. 140); Justin Martyr (ca. 100); Taitian (ca. 165); Athenagoras of Athens (ca. 180); Theophilus of Antioch (ca. 185); Melito of Sardis (ca. 171); Polycrates of Ephesus (ca. 125); Irenaeus of Lyon (ca. 140); Minucius Felix (ca. 218); Tertullian (ca. 155); Clement of Alexandria (ca. 150); Origen (ca. 185); Cornelius (ca. 251); Cyprian of Carthage (ca. 258); Firmilian of Caesarea (ca. 268), and so forth.

Never, ever has the acceptance of homosexual acts been accepted in the early Church!

Philosophy likewise is clear. To put it bluntly a male's genitals were not created for another male, and a male's sexual organ certainly has no place in any male body! The male and female organs are complementary, just as the psychological distinctions between males and females are complementary. The homosexual act is a sex act which is contrary to the act's purpose and completely closed off to life.

Because of the nature of males and females, the sexual act is unitive and procreative. Homosexual acts are neither unitive nor procreative, and thus are a direct attack on the dignity of the sanctity of the sexual act.

In pagan society homosexual activity was common and even practiced as part of many cults. Those who have taken college courses in Greek and Latin Classics have been shocked by the open discussion of homosexual activity and even more shockingly pedophilia.

During the period of the early Church, the distinction between homosexual activity and homosexual orientation was not made, being that it was so closely associated with paganism. It is only with the Church's correct interpretation, guided by the Holy Spirit, that the distinction between orientation and activity was made.

The Church makes it clear that a person's orientation is not sinful. As the *Catechism* states: Homosexuals "must be accepted with respect, compassion, and sensitivity. Every sign of unjust discrimination in their regard should be avoided. These persons are called to fulfill God's will in their lives and, if they are Christians, to unite to the sacrifice of the Lord's Cross the difficulties they may encounter from their condition" (CCC 2358). The Catechism goes on to say: "Homosexual persons are called to chastity. By virtue of self-mastery that teach them inner freedom, at times by the support of disinterested friendship, by prayer and sacramental grace, they can and should gradually and resolutely approach Christian perfection" (2359).

Never has the Christian community accepted homosexual activity until the twentieth century, and never has an active homosexual been proposed for ordination to the office of Bishop until the twenty-first century.

19

Child Abuse

Society bears the scars of the abuse of children. Two out of every three prisoners convicted of first-degree murder have histories of child abuse (U.S. Department of Justice, 2001). Prostitutes and juvenile delinquents also report histories of child abuse (Ibid.).

Society is wounded by an unimaginable number of individuals walking around who are suffering from various forms of pathological disorders due to such abuse.

When first investigating the issue of child abuse, one is tempted to say that our modern society is experiencing an epidemic of child abuse. In terms of sexual child abuse, it is reported that 1,100 children are abused every day, 400,000 every year. In our society, one in four girls, and one in seven boys are sexually abused before the age of eighteen. Fifty to seventy percent of sexual abuse is perpetuated on children by neighbors, friends and acquaintances. Thirty to fifty percent of sexual abuse is perpetuated on children by parents and relatives (National Center on Child Abuse and Neglect, 2001).

Sexual abuse of children cuts across all boundaries. One's economic level, race, ethnic heritage and religious faith have no bearing on the sexual abuse of children.

Parents, relatives, teachers, priests, ministers, rabbis are all part of the tragedy of sexual abuse.

While at first glance it may appear that our society is suffering from an increasing epidemic of child abuse, the reality, perhaps, is that society is not so much experiencing an epidemic of child abuse as it is experiencing the light of Christ uncovering the hidden evils that families and institutions have kept secret for so many years. What was once hidden is now coming to light.

When the dignity due to every person is not taken seriously then evil is bound to follow. When one fails to recognize life at its first moments, at conception, then is it so much a surprise that the dignity of persons can be assaulted? Child abuse is a direct attack on the individual's dignity as a child of God. It is a direct attack on a child who is the "image and likeness of God," the temple of grace, the temple of the Trinity.

May society always remember the words of Christ who reminded all that whoever harms a "little one," will have to pay a great price, for as he said: "It would be better for a person to have a millstone put around his neck and be thrown into the sea than to harm a little one" (Lk. 17:2).

Those in society who violate the boundaries of sacredness are called to turn themselves into the proper authorities, enter into treatment, seek God's forgiveness, and do acts of penance and reparation.

For those in authority who move child abusers from one area to another in the hope that all will just go away, they too must answer to the law and to God for failing to respect the dignity of the people they have been entrusted to shepherd.

The Church and our society in general have been slow to recognize this need for honesty and integrity in dealing with such issues as child abuse.

We thank God that the Holy Father and the bishops of the world are now taking an active role in seeking to purify the priesthood and society of the evil of child abuse.

20

Modern Comprehensive Sex Education and the Fall of Western Civilization

"Sexual science is of two kinds, that which is used for controlling or overcoming the sexual passion, and that which is used to stimulate and feed it. Instruction in the former is as necessary a part of a child's education, as the latter is harmful and dangerous, and fit, therefore, only to be shunned. The sex education that I stand for must have for its object the conquest and sublimation of the sex passion. Such education should automatically serve to bring home to children the essential distinction between man and brute, to make them realize that it is man's special privilege and pride to be gifted with the faculties of head and heart both, that he is a thinking no less than feeling animal, and to renounce the sovereignty of reason over the blind instincts is, therefore, to renounce a man's estate. In man, reason quickens and guides the feeling; in brutes, the soul lies ever dormant" (Wisdom for All Times: Mahatma Gandhi and Pope Paul VI on Birth Regulation).

—*Gandhi*

The sex education programs found in schools today have left the world a legacy of sexual brutes, fostering large masses of individuals, if not an entire generation, incapable of authentically loving.

There are essentially three types of sex education programs competing for acceptance in our culture. One is referred to as chastity education, another as biological sex education, and a final as comprehensive sex education.

Chastity Sex Education

Chastity sex education is that which recognizes the uniqueness of individuals and fosters authentic sexual integrity and authentic love. It fosters self-mastery and the most intimate nature of the human person. It is only through chastity sex education that one can experience real love and the gifts that flow from fidelity.

The reality is that one either controls one's sexual drive or one is controlled by it. As the 1995 Vatican document *The Truth and Meaning of Human Sexuality* states:

"If the person is not the master of self—through the virtues and, in a concrete way, through chastity—he or she lacks that self-possession which makes self-giving possible. Chastity is the spiritual power which frees love from selfishness and aggression…Chastity is the joyous affirmation of someone who knows how to live self-giving, free from any form of self-centered slavery…Either man governs his passions and finds peace, or he lets himself be dominated by them and becomes unhappy" (16, 17, 18).

"Chastity is not to be understood as a repressive attitude. On the contrary, chastity should be understood rather as the purity and temporary stewardship of a precious and rich gift of love, in view of the self-giving realized in each person's specific vocation. Chastity is thus the spiritual energy capable of defending love from the perils of selfishness and aggressiveness, and is able to advance it toward its full realization" (14).

Those who cannot master chastity will never be able to master fidelity and authentic self-giving for they will be slaves to their passions. They will never grasp the meaning of authentic family life, of authentic love and virtue and the respect for God's gift of sexuality and life. They will never be able to understand the intrinsic spirituality of the sex act.

The consequences of failing to foster chastity and self-mastery is the relinquishing of one's sexual energies to one's uncontrolled passions. This leads to the use of contraceptives (including abortifacients), divorce, abortion, child abuse, and perversions of all kinds. It leads to the disintegration between the body and soul, the physical and the spiritual. Is it any wonder that suicide has become an epidemic in our culture?

Biological and Comprehensive Sex Education

Biological sex education focuses on the purely biological functioning of the reproductive system with no regard to the spiritual. It is secular and atheistic or agnostic in approach.

Closely related to this, is the more hideous form of sex education known as comprehensive sex education. This has become the leading sex education program in the public schools.

Building upon the purely biological, the comprehensive sex education program's philosophy is essentially as follows: "If it is between two consenting adults, it is acceptable." There is no right or wrong. There is no moral value system. There is no spiritual dimension to the person. There is no interest in interpersonal relationships or chastity skills. The person is an organism, like any other. One is an animal like any other, and thus one can for all practical purposes act like any other animal.

This is the philosophy that has conquered our culture and our school systems. And so what do the public school textbooks teach? Premarital sex, open marriages or free unions, group sex, homosexuality, bisexuality, sadomasochism, incest, bestiality, masturbation, sex with inanimate objects, etc., are all discussed without any moral significance. Birth control, abortion, sterilization, and so forth, are discussed without any value attached to them.

This philosophy says, "No sex act is immoral." It says, "No lifestyle must be judged."

What has this philosophy done to our culture? (cf. Clowes, *Facts of Life; Bureau of Census; Statistical Abstract; Index of Leading Cultural Indicators*)

- Despite the pushing of contraceptives, abortions have increased from 200,000 to 1.4 million per year since 1960.

- Cohabitation has increased from 500,000 to 4 million.

- Divorce has increased from 400,000 to 1.2 million per year.

- Single-parent families have risen from 9 to 32 percent.

- Illegitimate births have increased from 200,000 to 1.5 million per year.

- Teenage pregnancy has increased from 30 to 110 per 1000 girls annually.

- Sexually transmitted diseases have increased 245 percent since 1960.

- More than 400,000 people have died from AIDS.

- Child abuse has increased 286 percents since 1960.

- Crime rates have increased by 510 percent.

When sex is divorced from its spiritual dimension, it lowers the person to the level of the brute, the animal. One either controls one's sexual drive or one is controlled by it!

Is it any wonder that Christendom is no longer? Is it any wonder that secularism, paganism or heathenism is on the rise?

If we do not respond to the forces of evil and take control of our schools, evil will prevail and our culture will die.

"In man, reason quickens and guides the feeling; in brutes, the soul lies ever dormant."

—Gandhi

21

Preferential Option for the Poor

"It is a poverty to decide that a child must die so that you may live as you wish."
—*Blessed Mother Teresa of Calcutta*

What Mother Teresa has said about abortion can very well be said about the hungry, the poor and the homeless around the world.

It is so easy for us to harden our hearts to the plight of the less fortunate (cf. Ps. 95). Yet the Gospel and the Catechism of the Catholic Church continue to remind us of the need to love our neighbor, and to have a preferential option or love for the poor (CCC 2448; *Libertatis conscientia*, 68).

In the United States, on any given day, four million children under the age of twelve and twenty-seven million adults go to bed hungry. On any given night, 500,000 to 700,000 people in the richest country in the world are homeless. Forty-four million lack health care insurance (U.S. Bureaus of Census; CCHIP).

In terms of world statistics, 30,000 to 40,000 people die of hunger every day. One in ten children dies before the age of five from malnutrition. Eight hundred million suffer malnutrition every day. Over 30,000 children die every day from preventable diseases such as diarrhea, malaria or from poor sanitary conditions. One hundred million people are homeless in the world. Eight hundred and eighty-eight million lack health care. The wealthiest fifth of the world's population consumes an astonishingly eighty-six percent of all goods and services, while the poorest fifth consumes one percent (UNICEF; Food for the Hungry; Food and Agriculture Organization of the United States).

Helping the needy is not as much an act of charity as it is a demand for justice (CCC 2446). It is an act of justice that has always been part of the Church's teachings (cf. Mt. 25:31-46; 5:42; 6:2-4; 8:20; 10:8; Lk. 6:20-22; Mk. 12:41-44; Jas. 2:13-16; 5:1-6; Eph. 4:28; cf. 1 Jn. 3:17). As St. John Chrysostom (d. 407) explains: "Not to enable the needy to share in our goods is to steal from them and deprive them of life (*Hom. In Lazaro*, 2,5: PG 48, 992). Blessings are to be shared.

Isolation is not part of Catholic tradition or spirituality. Christ calls us to be his ears, his eyes, his hands, his feet, and his voice in a world crying for him.

The Church, the body of Christ, demands us that we build a world where a solidarity of nations can be established to eliminate hunger, poverty, and homelessness (CCC 2438). It demands of us that we aid in the moral, cultural, and economic development of countries (CCC 2438; 2440). This is a grave and unavoidable responsibility for the wealthiest nations (CCC 2439). This is a grave and unavoidable responsibility for each and every one of us who call ourselves Christian: "How can God's love survive in a man who has enough of this world's goods yet closes his heart to his brother when he sees him in need" (1 Jn. 3:17)? May the Lord have mercy on our souls if we remain silent and inactive.

22

Health Care, A Basic Right

My father died in 1980, next to his car, in the streets of Los Angeles at the young age of fifty-two from a massive heart attack. The sad reality is that he did not have to die in this manner. My father was the victim of a health care system that is too often profit-oriented as opposed to person-oriented. He died because he was unable to find health insurance coverage for a pre-existing heart condition.

He needed heart bypass surgery, but no insurance company would insure him because the treatment for his heart condition would entail long-term financial loss.

I wish this were an unusual case.

Unfortunately, I have seen too many people die or become seriously ill unnecessarily because of a lack of health insurance or poor health insurance coverage.

In the United States, 8.5 million children and 39.3 million adults are without health insurance (U.S. Census Bureau, 2000).

In the wealthiest nation the world has ever seen, this is not acceptable. The providing of health care to all citizens in the United States is a basic requirement of a civilized society (CCC 2288). Pope John Paul II in his encyclical letter *Laborem Exercens* reminds the nations of the world that health care "should be easily available for people and that as far as possible it should be cheap or even free of charge" (19:5).

It is not the role of the Church to say *how* health care is to be provided. That is the role of enlightened politicians. However, it is very much the role of the Church to say that health care *must* be provided.

The bishops of the United States powerfully remind us of our call as Christians when they state: "In a world characterized by growing prosperity for some and pervasive poverty for others, Catholic teaching proclaims that a basic moral test is how our most vulnerable members are faring. In a society marred by deepening divisions between rich and poor, our tradition recalls the story of the Last Judgment (Mt. 25:31-46) and instructs us to put the needs of the poor vulnerable first" (USCCB, Social Development and World Peace).

How are our most vulnerable members without health care faring? What can we do to help?

23

Overpopulation, An Evil Myth

The idea that the world is overpopulated is a myth that the wealthy nations of the world and those with pro-abortion and pro-contraceptive agendas seek to promote. The wealthy nations seek to keep their standard of living up at the cost of the poor: the wealthiest fifth of the world's population consumes astonishingly eighty-six percent of all the goods and services, while the poorest fifth consumes one percent, according to UNICEF.

The pharmaceutical companies and Planned Parenthood, the world's leading abortion provider, have tremendous profits at stake in promoting the overpopulation myth. Their agenda is quite simple: contraception, abortion, sterilization.

Alan Guttmacher, the former director of the International Planned Parenthood Federation, made that agenda quite clear when he stated: "[Our objective is] compulsory sterilization and compulsory abortion."

Planned Parenthood—which perhaps has the greatest to gain from this myth—is not shy in using deceptive tactics, such as the one they used in a 1985 campaign: "The Human Race Has 35 Years Left: After That People Will Start Eating Plankton, Or People."

When one worships the god of money, innocents die!

Let us look at the real facts. If you took the entire population of the world, you could fit it comfortably into the state of Texas, with no greater population density than New Jersey. According to the U.S. Printing Office the world population in the year 2001 was 6.15 billion with a growth rate of .02 percent. Since 1900, food production has exceeded population increases. According to the United Nations' Population Information Network, the world's population will grow to 7.3 billion by the year 2040 and then level off.

While it is true that the population in so-called "third world" countries is increasing, the population in many countries in so-called "first world" countries is on the decline. In Italy, the birth rate does not equal the death rate, thus failing to even reach the level of replacement.

The fact that the world's population is in no danger of overpopulating the earth or in over-consuming the world's resources, does not mean that everything is okay.

Much of the population control being done in the world is not through Natural Family Planning and economic and industrial development, but through the evil means of abortion, sterilization, and contraception.

Furthermore, when we look below the surface of the distribution of resources in the world, we see a great imbalance, which leads to grave injustices. We see that 30,000 to 40,000 people die of hunger every day. One in ten children dies before the age of five from malnutrition. Eight hundred million suffer malnutrition every day. Over 30,000 children die every day from preventable diseases such as diarrhea, malaria, or from poor sanitary conditions. One hundred million people are homeless in the world. Eight hundred and eighty million lack health care.

In the name of combating hunger and population control, people who support abortion, contraception and sterilization are people that often misunderstand the poorest of the poor. Couples in the so-called "third world" have large families (i.e., five or more children) not out of ignorance but out of necessity. In the West we have social security and a pension plan when we retire. In the "third world" social security is found not in a check but in a couple's children. Since one out of ten children die before the age of five in these poorest of poor countries, a couple's only means of survival into old age (when they can no longer work the fields, etc.) is to have children to take care of them.

The more children one has the greater chance that some will survive to take care of them.

The wealthy countries must be willing to help in the development of the less fortunate nations, and they must be willing to share their excess of resources. As was mentioned before, the wealthiest fifth of the world's population consumes astonishingly eighty-six percent of all the goods and services, while the poorest fifth consumes one percent, according to UNICEF. A more generous heart is needed, even if our standard of living decreases. As Mother Teresa of Calcutta said: "It is a poverty to decide that a child must die so that we may live as we wish."

What then is the answer? When Margaret Sanger, the founder of Planned Parenthood, attempted to introduce contraceptives into India, Mahatma Gandhi reprimanded Sanger by pointing to the reality that what India needed was not contraceptives but "the proper land system, better agriculture and supplementary industry." If this was done, Gandhi continued, "India would be capable of supporting twice as many people."

The Holy Father, John Paul II, in his work *Evangelium Vitae*, summed up the Catholic teaching on population management and authentic development: "Governments and various national agencies must above all strive to create economic, social, public health and cultural conditions which will enable married couples to make their choices about procreation in full freedom and with genuine responsibility (i.e., using natural family planning). They must make efforts to ensure greater opportunities and a fairer distribution of wealth so that everyone can share equitably in the goods of creation. Solutions must be sought on the global level by establishing a true economy of communion and sharing of goods, in both the national and international order. This is the only way to respect the dignity of persons and families, as well as the authentic cultural patrimony of peoples" (91).

24

Legitimate War

Terrorism is a new way of waging war. The first impulse that engulfs us as human beings during terrorist attacks is the desire for revenge and retribution. But we as Christians, in times of difficulty, are called to calm down and allow the Spirit to enlighten us so as to act in a way that is in conformity with Christ and his Church.

In a spirit of prudence, the Church affirms the legitimate right to self-defense and war: "The legitimate defense of persons and societies is not an exception to the prohibition against the murder of the innocent that constitutes intentional killing" (CCC 2263).

"Legitimate defense can be not only a right but a grave duty for someone responsible for another's life, the common good of the family or the state" (CCC 2265). "Governments cannot be denied the right of lawful self-defense, once all peace efforts have failed" (GS 79,4). In fact, governments are often called to war for the betterment and the good of the world.

Recourse to war is permissible when the following conditions are met (2309; 2313-2314; ST II-II, 64,7):

1. The cause must be just.

2. All means of avoiding war or ending aggression must be seen to be "impractical and ineffective."

3. There must be an adequate prospect for success in putting an end to the aggression or evil.

4. The use of weaponry must be used with prudence. They must not "produce evils and disorders graver than the evil to be eliminated."

5. Every act of self-defense or war that is aimed at the indiscriminate destruction of whole cities is prohibited. Non-combatants must never be targeted.

Acts of terrorism remind us of the challenge of peace that we as Catholics are faced with. Hostilities, excessive economic inequalities, contempt and distrust for persons, and unbending ideologies are all part of the injustices that ferment war. What is needed is a spiritual renewal throughout the world, a renewal that fosters solidarity and a sense of universal cooperation among nations. All nations are called to a spirit of brotherhood and a desire for a universal common good. Social structures, attitudes, and hearts must change (GS 83-90). Unless we take up this challenge for peace, the world will inevitably enter a new dark age. Recent events have pointed to this sad reality.

25

The Death Penalty, Yesterday and Today

Punishment for criminal offenses has traditionally emphasized the importance of justice, retribution, deterrence and the protection of society. In terms of the death penalty, the key principle has always been the protection of society.

In describing the Church's position on the death penalty, the *Catechism of the Catholic Church* explains: "If nonlethal means are sufficient to defend and protect people's safety from the aggressor, authority will limit itself to such means, as these are more in keeping with the concrete conditions of the common good and more in conformity with the dignity of the human person" (CCC 2267).

Many people who read this passage often scratch their heads while saying: "How can this be? Isn't this the Church that has affirmed and often promoted the death penalty for centuries? What is going on?"

At first glance there may appear to be an inconsistency in the Church's current teaching on the death penalty, but in reality the Church's teaching has remained absolutely consistent.

The change in the Church's position is not due to a change in the theology as much as to developments in the ways of protecting and defending the common good of society.

Prior to the nineteenth century, violently dangerous criminals were dealt with by means of execution or exile (which was essentially another form of capital punishment due to the atrociously harsh conditions associated with it).

The infrastructure of society prior to the nineteenth century was incapable of dealing with long-term incarceration; hence, those who posed a serious threat to society, such as the criminally insane, needed to be taken out of society for the protection of the common good, and the only means available, for all practical purposes, during this period in history was the death penalty (Ives, *A History of Penal Methods*).

By the late nineteenth century and early twentieth century, developments in the structure and organization of society as well as enlightened thought led to the possibility of incarcerating individuals for life, thereby eliminating the moral justification for the death penalty. As Pope John Paul II explains in *Evangelium Vitae*: "Today...as a result of steady improvements in the organization of the penal system [the justification for the death penalty is] practically non-existent."

Justice without mercy is cruelty. Christian justice demands that we be protected from violent criminals, and Christian mercy demands that we forgive the unforgivable and hope for the hopeless. As long as there is life, there is the possibility for repentance and conversion. There is always hope. Death extinguishes hope and any possibility of conversion. If Jesus would not pull the switch or inject a person with heart stopping chemicals, why should we? Let society imprison the dangerously uncontrollable for the remainder of their lives, and let people of faith pray for their conversion. Let us remember that "whoever brings back a sinner from the error of his way will save his soul from death and will cover a multitude of sins," and let us also remember that there is "more joy in heaven over one sinner who repents than over ninety-nine righteous persons who need no repentance" (Jms. 5:20; 5:7).

In a modern, civilized society, the death penalty has no place.

26

Catholic Social Justice

Christians are called to a communion of persons, in imitation of our God. Because of this call, one is held to the demands of justice and peace in conformity with right-reason and divine wisdom (CCC 2419). One is called to defend the dignity of the person as the image and likeness of his or her maker.

The Church is obligated to make judgments of economic and social matters when the souls of individuals are at stake. All aspects of life in the social and economic dimension are to be ordered to the eternal destiny of people.

The following points are central to Catholic social justice:

- *"Any system in which social relationships are determined entirely by economic factors is contrary to the nature of the human person and his acts" (CA, 35).*

- *"A theory that makes profit the exclusive norm and ultimate end of economic activity is morally unacceptable. The disordered desire for money cannot but produce perverse effects. It is one of the causes of the many conflicts which disturb the social order" (GS 63,3; LE 7; 20; CA 35).*

- *"A system that subordinates the basic rights of individuals and of groups to the collective organization of production is contrary to human dignity. Every practice that reduces persons to nothing more than a means of profit enslaves man, leads to idolizing money, and contributes to the spread of atheism. You cannot serve God and mammon" (GS 65, 2; Mt. 6:24; Lk. 16:13).*

- *"The Church has rejected the totalitarian and atheistic ideologies associated in modern times with communism or socialism. She has likewise refused to accept, in the practice of capitalism, individualism and the absolute primacy of the law of the marketplace over human labor. Regulating the economy solely by centralized planning perverts the basis of social bonds; regulating it solely by the law of the marketplace fails social justice, for there are many human needs which cannot be satisfied by the market. Reasonable regulation of the marketplace and economic initiatives, in keeping with a just hierarchy of val-*

ues and a view to the common good, is to be commended" (CA 10; 13; 34; 44).

The rich nations have a responsibility for the poorer nations in a spirit of solidarity and charity.

27

Workers' Rights

Providing for the needs of workers is a fundamental right in all civilizations. Providing for the needs of workers must be in accordance to the moral law and right reason.

Work is a duty (cf. 1 Thess. 4:11; 2 Thess. 3:10) that honors the Creator and by its nature should be redemptive (cf. Gen. 3:14-19) and directed toward the justification of the person.

Workers' rights should include the following (cf. CCC 2426f):

1. Workers have the right to employment.

2. Workers have the right to a sufficient and just wage to provide for the material, social, cultural and spiritual welfare of one's life, one's family, and the common good of one's community.

3. The good of workers must not be infringed upon at the expense of profit.

4. All workers have a right to employment without discrimination.

5. Conflicts should be resolved by just negotiation with the dignity of all involved respected. In the event of an impasse, the right to *strike* for a proportionate benefit must be assured. Violence, however, is not to be resorted to.

6. A worker has the right to social security benefits, public services, and freedom of movement in jobs.

Providing for the needs of workers is a fundamental right in all civilizations. Providing for the needs of workers must be in accordance with the moral law and right reason.

28

Concluding Remarks

The theologian Jules Girardi, in summarizing why so many fail to believe in Christ, explained, "The scandal of 'believers' is not chiefly that of some crime or other, rather it is that Christianity does not startle the world."

Gandhi once mentioned that he never became a Christian because he never met one.

While we clearly find flaws in such statements, and rightly so, we must however ask ourselves whether we are doing our part to startle the world? Are we making our presence known?

The existentialist philosopher Albert Camus, while standing over the crushed body of a young boy, turned to his friend and said while pointing to the sky: "You see, the sky is dumb." Are we there to answer a Camus? Are we there to point to the way, the truth, and the life? The Jesuit theologian Karl Rahner once said: "The devout Christian of the future will either be a 'mystic,' one who has 'experienced' something, or he will cease to be anything at all." We as Christians are called to be different, to be recognizably different. May no one mistake who we are.

When we look to the media, we see so much confusion in the world. We see the Gospel values being undermined in subtle and often overt ways. We see a world that is becoming more and more foreign to the Gospel message. We see violence and injustices of all kinds—abortion, euthanasia, cloning, embryonic stem cell research, racism, prejudice, promiscuity, and so forth. The world is crying for Christ, crying for authentic love, crying for a direction in life. We see a world in so much need of healing.

To be a Christian today is not an easy task. But just as we wave the American flag around, we must wave the Christian flag around.

We must make our presence known. Just as we are not afraid to be known as Americans, we must not be afraid to be known as Catholics.

We live in a world we are fully aware of, a world with many distinct visions of reality, and we recognize that one way or another we will accept one vision of reality. It is inescapable. What lenses will we wear? The lenses we wear will influence our understanding of reality and our response to reality.

May we always renew our commitment to see the world through the lenses, the eyes, of Christ. To do such is to see reality the way it authentically is.

Let us seek to recognize that God sees his Son in each and every one of us; that we are created in his image and likeness; and that we bear the handprint of God in our very being. If we can do so, we will truly startle the world for Christ. We will startle the world for the Gospel of Life.

Epilogue:
In Memoriam

◆

(1930–2002)

John Hrach was a retired postal worker, a veteran of the Korean War, a member of the Knights of Columbus, a parishioner at Saint Anastasia Church, and a legendary prayer warrior and counselor for the cause of life.

John would begin his day by attending Mass and being nourished by the bread of eternal life, the Body, Blood, Soul, and Divinity of Christ. From there he went to the local abortion facility to pray the Rosary and sidewalk counsel anyone who would listen. He prayed through rain, hail, heavy winds, frost, unbearable heat and bone-chilling cold. Nothing would prevent him from standing up for life and the culture of life, not even cancer.

John was diagnosed with cancer in the summer of 2000. Yet this would not stop his steadfastness. He would take his chemo treatment and blood transfusions in the morning, offer up his sufferings for the unborn, and then would go directly to the abortion facility. Amidst his weakness and ever-consuming cancer, John was a shining light of hope for the cause of life. As he was dying, he was bringing life to others.

On Friday, March 22, John was nearing the end of his earthly pilgrimage at Hospice of the Treasure Coast. He had but a few hours to live. John asked for the "last rites." Father Thomas Euteneuer of Human Life International administered the sacrament and told John that he was going to pray at the abortion facility on his behalf. John told Father Tom, "Don't worry, I'll be there with you all."

At 6 p.m. a woman entered the parking lot of the abortion clinic, glanced at the pro-life prayer evangelists, and came out to talk to one of the sidewalk counselors. After much prayer, reflection, and talking, the woman decided to keep her baby and left for home happy and at peace. It was 6:30 p.m.

John died exactly at 6:30 p.m., at the very moment the woman changed her mind. With his last breath of prayer John had saved one more child and one more woman from the psychological trauma of abortion.

John Hrach was known as the "Rock" for his faithfulness and dedication to the cause of life. It is quite appropriate that a memorial was dedicated to him on the very spot he stood for so many years.

Well done good and faithful servant. Your reward will be great in heaven.

John Hrach, pray for us!

Appendix A

The Ten Commandments and Their Implications

✦

(CCC 2084–2550)

1. The first commandment forbids acts of superstition, divination, magic, and all forms of sacrilege. It forbids acts of idolatry such as the worship of money, power, fame, and all sorts of "worldly" accomplishments. It forbids atheism and agnosticism, for they are nothing other than the hidden or subconscious worship of self.

2. The second commandment demands a respect for the sacredness of the Lord's name. Acts of blasphemy, the taking of false oaths, and acts of perjury are strictly forbidden.

3. The third commandment is a summons to keep the Lord's Day a holy day. It demands the faithful attendance of Sunday Mass, and an attitude of profound worship. It is a time to spend with God and to abstain from any work that distracts from authentically consecrating Sunday as a precious day of love of God and love of neighbor. One seeks comfort, but one also seeks to be challenged to grow.

4. The fourth commandment demands the authentic honoring of father and mother. This means obedience, respect, gratitude, and the repaying of love for love.

5. The fifth commandment is an affirmation of the dignity of life, of not murdering. Unjust war, direct abortions, the use of contraceptives, suicide, and intentional euthanasia are all forbidden by this commandment.

6. The sixth commandment is a command that demands fidelity. Any act which is contrary to the dignity of chastity, such as fornication, adultery, polygamy, open or free marriages, divorce, homosexual and bisexual acts, masturbation, pornography, are forbidden. The sixth commandment is a call to authentic sexual integration.

7. The seventh commandment is a prohibition against stealing. It is characteristic of a lack of charity and injustice. Often stealing is done in subtle ways: For example, on the part of employers in a business a violation of the seventh commandment is often exemplified by the mistreatment of workers through unfair wages, lack of health benefits, and lack of retirement benefits. On the part of the employee this injustice and lack of charity is often seen in acts of laziness and all forms of lack of effort in the work environment.

8. The eighth commandment is a prohibition against bearing false witness against one's neighbor. Lying, duplicity, hypocrisy, dissimulation (that is, hiding under a false appearance), betrayal of confidences, calumny (character assassination), slander, and so forth are all acts contrary to the dignity of persons.

9. The ninth commandment is a prohibition against coveting one's neighbor's wife. This commandment calls one to live a life of decency and modesty. It is a call for purity of heart, intention, and vision.

10. The tenth commandment is a call to avoid coveting another's goods. It is a call to avoid avarice, envy, and all immoderate desires. It is a call to desire detachment of all that is contrary to the glory and honor of God. One is called to desire God above all.

Fulfilling the Commandments

[A lawyer asked Jesus:] "Teacher, which is the greatest commandment in the law?" And he said to him, "You shall love the Lord your God with all your heart, with all your soul, and with all your mind. This is the great and first commandment. And a second is like it. You shall love your neighbor as yourself. On these two commandments depend all the law and the prophets" (Matthew 22:37-40, RSV).

To authentically love is to fulfill and grasp the true intentions of the commandments. The "culture of life" and the roadmap to light, peace, and happiness is based on the fulfillment of these commandments.

APPENDIX B

Pro-Abortion, Pro-Choice as Unchristian

The following Scripture quotes and quotes from some of the earliest Christian writings point to the unchristian nature of abortion and pro-choice proponents (cf. Clowes, Facts of Life).

Scripture

"The children in Rebekah's womb jostled each other so much that she exclaimed, 'If this is to be so, what good will it do me!' She went to consult the Lord, and he answered her: 'Two nations are in your womb…" (Gen. 25:22-24).

"Before I formed you in the womb I knew you, before you were born I dedicated you, a prophet to the nations I appointed you" (Jeremiah 1:5).

"Thus says the Lord who made you, who formed you from the womb: Fear not, O Jacob, my servant whom I have chosen" (Isaiah 44:2; see v. 24).

"The Lord called me from birth, from my mother's womb he gave me my name" (Isaiah 49:2).

"Your hands have formed me and fashioned me; with skin and flesh you clothed me, with bones and sinews you knit me together" (cf. Job 10:8, 11).
"Did not he who made me in the womb make him? Did not the same One fashion us before our birth" (Job. 31:15).

"You formed my inmost being; you knit me in my mother's womb. I praise you, so wonderfully you made me, wonderful are your works! My very self you knew; my bones were not hidden from you, when I was being made in secret, fashioned as in the depths of the earth. Your eyes foresaw my actions; in your book all are written down; my days were shaped, before one came to be" (Psalm 139:13-16).

"Just as you know not how the breath of life fashions the human frame in the mother's womb, so you know not the work of God which he is accomplishing in the universe" (Ecclesiastes 11:5).

"When Elizabeth heard Mary's greeting, the infant leaped in her womb, and Elizabeth, filled with the Holy Spirit, cried out in a loud voice and said, 'Most blessed are you among women, and blessed is the fruit of your womb. And how does this happen to me that the mother of my Lord should come to me? For at the moment the sound of your greeting reached my ears, the infant in my womb leaped for joy" (Luke 1:41-44).

"Behold, Elizabeth, has conceived a son in her old age, and this is the sixth month for her..." (cf. Luke 1:36).

Other quotes worth reviewing: Genesis 16:2-4; 19:36-38; 21:1-18; 38; 50: 20; Exodus 21:22-25; Leviticus 19:14; Numbers 35:22-34; Deuteronomy 27:25; Jeremiah 7:6; 22:17; Isaiah 45:9-12; Psalm 94:9; 106:37-38; Proverbs 6:16-19; Ruth 4:18-22; Matthew 1:3; 18:10-14; Luke 3:33; 17:2; John 9:1-3; Acts 17:25-29; Romans 8:28.

Early Church Writings

"You shall not kill an unborn child or murder a newborn infant."

—*Didache*, II, 2 (ca. 65 AD)

"You shall love your neighbor more than your own life. You shall not slay the child by abortion."

—Barnabas, *Epistles*, II (ca. 70-138).

"For us murder is once and for all forbidden; so even the child in the womb, while yet the mother's blood is still being drawn on to form the human being, it is not lawful for us to destroy. To forbid birth is only quicker murder. He is a man, who is to be a man; the fruit is always present in the seed."

—Tertullian, 197, *Apologetics* (ca. 197)

"Those who use drugs to bring about an abortion commit murder and will have to give an account to God for their abortion."

—Athenagoras, *Legatio pro Christianis*, (ca. 177)

"There are women, who, by the use of medicinal potions, destroy the unborn life in their wombs, and murder the child before they bring it forth. These practices undoubtedly are derived from a custom established by your gods; Saturn, though he did not expose his sons, certainly devoured them."

—Minucius Felix, *Octavius* (ca. 200)

"If we would not kill off the human race born and developing according to God's plan, then our whole lives would be lived according to nature. Women who make use of some sort of deadly abortion drug kill not only the embryo but, together with it, all human kindness."

—Clement of Alexandria, *Christ the Educator, II* (ca. 150-220)

"Sometimes this lustful cruelty or cruel lust goes so far as to seek to procure baneful sterility, and if this fails the fetus conceived in the womb is in one way or another smothered or evacuated, in the desire to destroy the offspring before it has life, or if it already lives in the womb, to kill it before it is born."

—Augustine, *De Nuptius et Concupiscus* (354-430)

"Some unmarried women, when they are with child through sin, practice abortion by the use of drugs. Frequently they kill themselves and are brought before the ruler of the lower world guilty of three crimes; suicide, adultery against Christ, and murder of an unborn child."

—Jerome, *Letter to Eustochium*, 22.13. (ca. 340-420)

"The hairsplitting difference between formed and unformed makes no difference to us. Whoever deliberately commits abortion is subject to the penalty for homicide."

—Basil the Great, *First Canonical Letter* (ca. 329-379)

To call oneself a Christian and pro-abortion or pro-choice is to promote an outrageous lie. To be indifferent or to vote for pro-choice or pro-abortion candidates is to betray one's Christianity. Those who betray their faith are worthy of the fires of hell.

APPENDIX C

Pro-Life Literature

Ashley, Benedict and Kevin O'Rourke. *Health Care Ethics: A Theological Analysis.* Washington: Georgetown University Press, 1996.

Ashley, Benedict. *Theologies of the Body: Humanist and Christian.* Braintree: Pope John Center, 1985.

Bohr, David. *Catholic Moral Tradition.* Huntington: Our Sunday Visitor, 1994.

Burke, Theresa with David C. Reardon. *Forbidden Grief: The Unspoken Pain of Abortion.* Springfield: Acorn Books, 2001.

Catechism of the Catholic Church. Washington: Libreria Editrice Vaticana, 2001. Particularly 1691–2550.

Clowes, Brian. *Catholics for a Free Choice Exposed.* Front Royal. Human Life International, 2001.

Clowes, Brian. *The Facts of Life: An Authoritative Guide to Life and Family Issues.* Front Royal: Human Life International, 2001.

Coyle, C.T. *Men and Abortion: A Path to Healing.* Belleville: Essence Publishing, 1999.

Demmer, Klaus. *Christian Marriage Today.* Washington: Catholic University Press, 1997.

Guitton, Stephanie and Peter Irons. *May it Please the Court: Arguments on Abortions.* New York: The New Press, 1995.

John Paul II. *The Gospel of Life*. New York: Random House, 1995.

John Paul II. *The Theology of the Body: Human Love in the Divine Plan*. Boston: Pauline Books and Media, 1997.

Kahlenborn, Chris. *Breast Cancer: Its Links to Abortion and the Birth Control Pill*. Dayton: One More Soul, 2000.

Klusendorf, Scott. *Pro-Life: A Step-by-Step to Making Your Case Persuasively*. Signal Hill: Stand to Reason Press, 2002.

Lash, Sybil. *Supreme Deception*. Lawrenceville, Sentinel Productions, 2002.

Lawler, Ronald. *Catholic Sexual Ethics*. Huntington: Our Sunday Visitor, 1985.

May, William. *Catholic Bioethics and the Gift of Human Life*. Huntington: Our Sunday Visitor, 2000.

Newman, Troy and Cheryl Sullenger. *Their Blood Cries Out*. Sacramento: Restoration Press, 2001.

Newman, Troy and Cheryl Sullenger. *Am I Now Your Enemy for Telling You the Truth?* Sacramento: Restoration Press, 2002.

Ney, Philip. *Deeply Damaged: An Explanation for the Profound Problems Arising from Aborting Babies and Abusing Children*. Pioneer Publishing, 1997.

Paul VI. *Humanae vitae*, in Austin Flannery, O.P., ed. *Vatican II: More Post Conciliar Documents*. Collegeville: The Liturgical Press, 1982.

Reardon, David. *Victims and Victors*. Springfield: Acorn Books, 2000.

S.C.D.F. *The Book 'Human Sexuality,'* in Austin Flannery, O.P., ed. *Vatican II: More Post Conciliar Documents*. Collegeville: The Liturgical Press, 1982.

S.C.D.F., *Haec sacra congregation*, in Austin Flannery, O.P., ed. *Vatican II: More Post Conciliar Documents*. Collegeville: The Liturgical Press, 1982.

S.C.D.F., *Jura et bona*, in Austin Flannery, O.P., ed. *Vatican II: More Post Conciliar Documents*. Collegeville: The Liturgical Press, 1982.

S.C.D.F., *Personae Humanae*, in Austin Flannery, O.P., ed. *Vatican II: More Post Conciliar Documents*. Collegeville: The Liturgical Press, 1982.

S.C.D.F. *Questio de abortu*, in Austin Flannery, O.P., ed. *Vatican II: More Post Conciliar Documents*. Collegeville: The Liturgical Press, 1982.

Schlossberg, Terry and Elizabeth Achtemeier. *Not My Own: Abortion and the Marks of the Church*, 1995.

Smith, Wesley. *Culture of Death: The Assault on Medical Ethics in America*. San Francisco: Encounter Books, 2000.

Stallsworth, Paul, ed. *Building a Ministry of Life*. Anderson: Bristol House, 2000.

Stallsworth, Paul, ed. *The Church and Abortion*. Nashville: Abingdon Press, 1993.

Stallsworth, Paul, ed. *The Right Choice*. Nashville: Abingdon Press, 1997.

Strahan, Thomas. *Detrimental Effects of Abortion*. Springfield: Acorn Books, 2001.

Tankard, Melinda. *Giving Sorrow Words: Women's Stories of Grief after Abortion*. Potts Point: Duffy and Snellgrove, 2000.

0-595-29779-X